BUSINESS
OF A
SPIRITUAL
MATTER

Advance Praise for
Business of a Spiritual Matter

"*Business of a Spiritual Matter* is a long-awaited gift and there is no one better gifted to serve as a guide than Gasby Brown. I know because I have had the privilege of teaching alongside her and learning from her."

—Dr. William Enright
Founding Karen Lake Buttrey Director Emeritus
Lake Institute on Faith & Giving

"*Business of a Spiritual Matter* serves as a much-needed, step-by-step guide for decision-makers in the nonprofit sector, specifically those in the faith-based arena. Author Gasby Brown brings a wealth of knowledge as an experienced consultant and advisor on how to effectively make a compelling case and position your organization in such a way that people will give freely as a result of proper preparation. Nonprofit organizations can't afford to overlook these important principles of charitable giving."

—John K. Jenkins, Sr.
Senior Pastor
First Baptist Church of Glenarden

"*Business of a Spiritual Matter* should be a mandatory training manual for every new nonprofit executive serious about leading her or his organization well. And yet, even this old(er) CEO easily found great value in this book. It couldn't have come at a better time!"

—David Staal
Former President & CEO
Kids Hope USA

"Gasby Brown is a well-known and highly respected practitioner and teacher of philanthropy. Her book, *Business of a Spiritual Matter: What All Leaders of Faith-Based Nonprofits Should Know*, is accessible to people in congregations, schools, and any faith-based nonprofit organization, as well as to those who offer professional guidance and expertise in every area of philanthropy. It can also become a valuable guide book for any and all who are considering a significant fund-raising endeavor. In fact, Gasby Brown has written a book which will make a major difference in philanthropy for years to come."

—The Rev. Dr. George B. Wirth
Pastor Emeritus, First Presbyterian Church Atlanta

BUSINESS
OF A
SPIRITUAL
MATTER

✝ ✡ ☪

What All Leaders of Faith-Based
Nonprofits Should Know

M. Gasby Brown

SelectBooks, Inc.
New York

This edition published by SelectBooks, Inc.
For information address SelectBooks, Inc., New York, New York.

First Edition
ISBN 978-1-59079-473-9

Library of Congress Cataloging-in-Publication Data

Names: Brown, M. Gasby, author.
Title: Business of a spiritual matter : what all leaders of faith-based
  nonprofits should know / M. Gasby Brown.
Description: First edition. | New York : SelectBooks, [2019] | Includes
  bibliographical references and index.
Identifiers: LCCN 2018055547 | ISBN 9781590794739 (pbk. : alk. paper)
Subjects: LCSH: Nonprofit organizations--Management. | Faith-based human
  services.
Classification: LCC HD62.7 .B78 2019 | DDC 658/.048--dc23 LC record
available at https://lccn.loc.gov/2018055547

Manufactured in the United States of America
10 9 8 7 6 5 4 3 2 1

This book is dedicated to the memory of

The Reverend Wesley Gasby, Jr., and Stella Gasby...
it all started with you.

Kenny, your support and encouragement have meant everything.

Janine, Toi, Damon, Rico, Norman, Brandis, Jamal, Eli,
Whitney and Artis;
all of you have inspired me.

Bob, Sandy, Kim, Malcolm, and the Brown crew...
your faith has been invaluable.

Doris, Cecelia, my posse of friends, and many supporters...
you know how important you are to my life.
Also to the women and men who do good
by leading faith-based organizations.

Contents

Preface

Business of a Spiritual Matter was birthed out of a need. As a practitioner and teacher of philanthropy, I have seen too many parachurch nonprofit organizations using the wrong model to run their operations. In many instances, because their mission and operation were tied to faith and churches, they have operated in a "let's take a collection" mentality resulting in a "scarcity" mindset rather than an "abundance" fundraising approach. If they had a philanthropic strategy, it was much too casual. While their missions were wonderful, the impact of their work was not going to be realized by operating in this fashion.

What I observed concerned me and grieved my spirit. So, what does one do when there is a problem of this kind? I could continue to observe and shake my head in dismay, or do something to help. My choice was clear: provide a tool that could help. If not now, then when? *Business of A Spiritual Matter* is meant to be a primer, if you will, to help you navigate the nonprofit sector while doing your important work. This book will help you lay the right foundation. In Matthew 7:24–27 (NKJV) it is said:

> *(24)* Anyone who listens to my teaching and follows it is wise, like a person who builds a house on solid rock. *(25)* Though the rain comes in torrents and the floodwaters rise and the winds beat against that house, it won't collapse because it is built on bedrock. *(26)* But anyone who hears my teaching and doesn't obey it is foolish, like a

person who builds a house on sand.   *(27)* When the rains and floods come and the winds beat against that house, it will collapse with a mighty crash.

This book is a guide for leaders, staff, and volunteers that will engender confidence through knowledge—the stability for a strong foundation. That's why I have provided questions and action steps for each chapter. Therefore, whether you have operated a faith-based organization for a long time, or you are just starting one, this book is for you. I have concentrated on the Abrahamic faiths: Christianity, Judaism, and Islam, with an emphasis on biblical scriptures as a guide. My years of experience as a nonprofit leader and consultant have served to provide seasoned and empirical advice.

I recommend that you use *Business of a Spiritual Matter* as a workbook to make notes, think about action steps where appropriate, and meditate on the scriptures used to introduce each chapter.

It is often said that "knowledge is power," but I believe we should take the quote a step further: "Applied knowledge is true power." That's my challenge to you. Enjoy the journey.

Acknowledgments

There are so many people who are responsible for my evolution as a consultant to philanthropy and this book. People, who along my fundraising and philanthropic journey, believed in me and my future. They include Hugh B. Price, former president of the National Urban League (NUL), and the late Reginald Brack, former Chairman of Time Inc. and NUL Board Chair, where I cut my teeth on the relationships needed for effective fundraising. The late and great guru of philanthropy, Jerry Panas, who was my mentor in fundraising and inspired me in innumerable ways to be and do my best; Tim Seiler at The Fund Raising School (TFRS) at the Lilly Family School of Philanthropy, who taught me how to teach fundraising and become an academic in the field; William Enright, Founding Karen Lake Buttrey Director Emeritus of Lake Institute on Faith & Giving, whose incredible intellect, faith, and support have been a guiding light; Carole Pence, a consultant in her own right who encouraged me to join TFRS' faculty; the late Eleanor Gentry, president of the Gary, Indiana, Urban League who encouraged me to attend The Fund Raising School (even after I had raised millions of dollars) and realized that if I had this information earlier I would have raised even more; several of my colleagues at TFRS with whom I have taught and from whom I learned so much; and the current supportive TFRS leadership of Bill Stanczykiewicz; my treasured clients who have trusted and allowed me to share my expertise. My spiritual growth that has undergirded the premise of

Business of a Spiritual Matter is due to the teaching and preaching of John K. Jenkins, Sr., Senior Pastor, First Baptist Church of Glenarden; Jim Cymbala, Pastor, The Brooklyn Tabernacle; Calvin Butts, Senior Pastor, Abyssinian Baptist Church; the late Wyatt Tee Walker, Pastor, Canaan Baptist Church; the late Benjamin L. Hooks, and the late L.W. Craig, who were Pastors at Greater New Mt. Moriah Missionary Baptist Church. Rebecca Ballard, Mark Swartz, LaToya Henry, and Toni Jones who were wonderful in doing research and offering ideas that kept this book project afloat over the years. Thank you so very much for believing in my dream and making such a fundamental contribution to it. Molly Stern and Nancy Sugihara, wonderful editors at SelectBooks, thank you for your patience and precision. To Mary Spence who provided valuable administrative assistance in countless ways to move this book along, and, last but not least, thank you Holy Spirit, for putting this book in me to share with others.

Foreword

Several years ago I was leading a seminar for more than seventy faith-based nonprofits that needed to raise matching funds as part of a grant they had received from a foundation. One of the attendees, the CEO of a faith-based nonprofit, shared this story. As she was waiting to board her flight, she found herself talking with the local leader of the United Way. He inquired as to where she was going. She then described the purpose of the fundraising seminar she would be attending. A wow of surprise instantly rippled his face as he said: "Goodness gracious, if you religious people ever learn how to practice good fundraising and organizational principles, the rest of us will be in trouble."

Something is unique when it comes to fundraising for religious congregations and faith-based nonprofits. Only faith-based organizations can wrap fundraising principles in a compelling religious package. It has been my observation that faith communities frequently stumble when it comes to wedding their spiritual calling to good business and fundraising practices. Some simply ignore their religious roots and what it is that sets them apart from a purely secular organization. Others shun good organizational practices, believing that all they need to do is pray and God will provide. The upshot is that many faith-based nonprofits fail to realize their fundraising and missional potential.

Religious faith is a powerful motivator when it comes to charitable giving as donors seek to connect God to their giving. Research shows that the majority of donors give to organizations they perceive as having a religious or spiritual mission. Donors motivated by faith also want to know more about what you do; they want to hear your story as to "why you do what you do" and "how your spiritual calling shapes how you do what you do." Questions, the answers to which, lay bare the heart of a faith-based nonprofit.

In *Business of a Spiritual Matter* Gasby Brown builds a much-needed bridge between the spiritual and the secular, between fidelity to one's calling and the building of a transparent and trustworthy organization. In her book she engagingly provides the newest visionary with the tools needed in creating a nonprofit, building a board, and launching an annual giving program. She also gifts the more seasoned nonprofit leader with savvy insights when launching a capital campaign, choosing a consultant, creating a planned giving program, or approaching a foundation for a major gift.

I have found leaders of faith-based nonprofits to be eager learners. All they need are teachers to guide them as they learn to embrace with integrity both the secular and spiritual side of the nonprofit world. *Business of a Spiritual Matter* is a long-awaited gift, and there is no one better gifted to serve as a guide than Gasby Brown. I know because I have had the privilege of teaching alongside her and learning from her.

Dr. William Enright
Founding Karen Lake Buttrey Director Emeritus, Lake Institute on Faith & Giving
Former Senior Pastor of Second Presbyterian Church, Indianapolis

Chapter One

A Brief History of Faith-Based Organizations: American Giving

For inquire, please, of the former ages, and consider the things discovered by their fathers; For we were born yesterday, and know nothing, because our days on earth are a shadow. Will they not teach you and tell you and utter words from their heart?

—Job 8:8–10 (NKJV)

The nonprofit sector of the United States and its history of volunteerism are unlike any other. In fact, it may be the most expansive and robust in the world. Faith-based philanthropy is so deeply woven into America's fabric that it was established soon after the Puritans came to our shores in the early 1600s. Our country's philanthropic tradition continued and strengthened as the nation formed and developed. World War I, though devastating, created tremendous national unity throughout the United States. Wealthy industrialists and financiers have steered many of the most significant developments in philanthropy in the late twentieth and early twenty-first centuries. The rise of the internet has ushered in additional opportunities for charities.

Let's take a journey through time and note some of the key events that have helped form the unique culture of faith-based nonprofits, and focus particularly on the strong organizations that are present in American society today.

In the 1600s the English-educated Puritans who traversed the Atlantic to start anew brought the concept of the "university" to the colonies. In 1637 a certain Puritan named John Harvard came to New England to practice his faith in what he believed would be a simpler, purer style. Upon his death a year later, the wealthy Harvard willed half of his estate and his entire library to a college founded two years earlier by the Massachusetts Bay Colony. The college was consequently named after him in gratitude for his bequest, and just six years later Harvard University conducted America's first recorded fund-raising drive and created the first scholarship fund.

Saint George's Society of New York, one of the oldest charities in the United States, was created in 1770 to help impoverished colonists in New York. The issue of philanthropy for all Americans and the need for an organized system to channel charitable giving was furthered in 1835 when Alexis de Tocqueville completed *Democracy in America* in which he noted the American disposition to create and join voluntary associations that provided charitable relief to those in need. De Tocqueville recorded that at this time America did not have a wealthy class that could provide aid in times of distress, but instead had compassionate associations formed to assist those in need.

Faith-based philanthropy persistently grew and thrived throughout the 1800s, both before and after the Civil War. Many faith-based groups that were active in England reached the United States and flourished. Retired Boston sea captain Thomas Valentine Sullivan, inspired by the same type of work in England, helped form the first Young Men's Christian Association (YMCA) in 1851. In 1879 Eliza Shirley, who had left England to join her family in America, held the first meeting of the Salvation Army in Philadelphia, Pennsylvania. There was great enthusiasm surrounding this first meeting, and after a year an official group was sent from England to assist the work being done in the United States. In three years' time, despite initial resistance, the Salvation Army managed to expand to twelve states. Their work was so successful that in 1886 President Grover Cleveland welcomed a delegation of the Salvation Army into the White House.

The shape of philanthropy in the United States changed forever when Andrew Carnegie wrote "The Gospel of Wealth" in 1889 in which he set forth what we now know as the modern American notion of philanthropy. Carnegie advanced the idea that the rich should not simply leave their wealth to their families, but must administer it as a public trust in their lifetime. Driven strongly by his convictions, he formed the Carnegie Corporation of New York in 1911 for "the advancement and diffusion of knowledge and understanding" with an endowment of $135 million, which was about a fifth of the federal government's annual budget. Carnegie, leading his wealthy friends and colleagues by example, inspired others to do the same. In 1913 John D. Rockefeller Sr. founded the Rockefeller Foundation with a gift of $50 million to further "the well-being of mankind throughout the world."

Around the turn of the century, a number of the faith-based philanthropic organizations were formed in America that are still well known today. These organizations did not arrive from England, but were a product of American society. Volunteers of America was founded in 1896 by social reformers Ballington and Maud Booth who envisioned a movement dedicated to "reaching and uplifting" the American people. Volunteers of America pledged to go wherever, whenever, to do whatever was needed. In the early 1900s Volunteers of America moved into tenement districts to care for the poor and established the nation's first system of halfway houses for released prisoners. This period in time also saw the creation of Goodwill Industries in 1902, the Boy Scouts of America in 1910, and Catholic Charities in 1910. In 1914 the first community foundation, The Cleveland Foundation, was formed.

Eventually, there were tax implications for donors and charitable organizations alike who aimed to serve Americans in need. Many changes that were made to the tax code affected faith-based philanthropy in the twentieth century. In 1913 the Sixteenth Amendment legally established the federal income tax. The Revenue Act of 1913 included a list of the types of charitable organizations that were exempt from paying income tax. Three years later, the Revenue Act of 1916 established the estate tax. In 1917 laws surrounding income tax permitted Americans to deduct charitable contributions up to 15 percent of their income. This helped fund the country's participation in World War I and helped to encourage private philanthropy. That same year the American Red Cross asked for and received $100 million, which was at that time the largest amount raised by any voluntary organization.

In 1918 the American Red Cross successfully raised more than $400 million in connection with World War I. This was the first national fundraising campaign effort in the United States. In 1919 Harvard University used what is believed to be the first professional fundraising counsel to assist with its $14 million fund drive.

It was not until 1921 that Americans started receiving tax relief in exchange for personal giving. Congress first formally recognized private foundations in the tax code that same year. However, corporations did not receive tax benefits until after the Great Depression. In 1934 Congress amended the tax code to allow tax-exempt organizations to do some lobbying but banned them from engaging in political activity. Then, the Revenue Act of 1935 was passed to permit corporations to deduct charitable contributions up to 5 percent of their income.

CRISIS AND RESPONSE

The Great Depression was a time of struggle for so many Americans as well as a time in which a number of charities formed or reshaped their missions to meet the needs of the population. At this time, Volunteers of America rallied to assist the millions of struggling Americans. Their relief efforts included employment bureaus, woodyards, soup kitchens, and "Penny Pantries," where every food item cost one cent. In 1929 the Capuchin Province of St. Joseph, a faith-based group that began its Detroit ministry in 1883, started the Capuchin Soup Kitchen to assist with the devastating poverty caused by the Great Depression. Lines grew to over two thousand people for their day's single meal. Even Al Capone tried to alleviate hunger and poverty during the Great Depression; in 1930 he opened a free soup kitchen for people who had been thrown out of work.

In 1936 the Ford Foundation was created "to receive and administer funds for scientific, educational and charitable purposes, all for the public welfare." A year later President Roosevelt established the National Foundation for Infantile Paralysis, which was later named the March of Dimes.

Then came the Second World War. As the number of armed forces increased, President Roosevelt decided it would be best for private organizations to handle the recreation of the armed forces. In 1941 at the request of the president, the Salvation Army, YMCA, YWCA, National Catholic Community Service, National Travelers Aid Foundation, and National Jewish Welfare Board joined together to form the United Service Organizations (USO). During World War Two, Volunteers of America operated canteens, which provided lodging and breakfast for soldiers and sailors, as well as affordable housing and childcare for defense workers. They also held community salvage drives that collected materials for the war effort. Despite the war and needs on the home front, faith-based American charities were visionary and looked to help people in other countries. The Heifer Project International sent their first shipment of heifers to Puerto Rico in 1944.

In the second half of the twentieth century, faith-based organizations continued to thrive and also encouraged Americans to use their faith to help others throughout the world. One example is Habitat for Humanity. In 1965 Millard and Linda Fuller visited Koinonia Farm, a small Christian farming community in Maryland founded to promote racial reconciliation. The Fullers decided to leave a successful business and affluent life behind to begin a life of Christian service at Koinonia Farm. There, they developed the concept of "partnership housing," which centered on those in need of adequate shelter working side by side with volunteers to build "a simple, decent place to live," forming Habitat for Humanity's core values. In 1976, Habitat for Humanity was officially born.

The 1960s brought forth the creation of another type of non-profit structure that is commonly seen in the faith-based world today—the community development corporation (CDC). In 1966 Robert Kennedy toured the Bedford-Stuyvesant community in Brooklyn, New York. Haunted by the conditions he found, Kennedy secured passage of an amendment that allowed for the government to fund community development projects in urban poverty areas. In the wake of this law, the first community development corporation, the Bedford Stuyvesant Restoration Corporation, was created. Non-CDC faith-based philanthropic groups also focused on housing during this time. For example, in the 1970s Volunteers of America continued their housing mission by taking part in numerous federal housing programs. Private philanthropic groups provided some support to CDCs, and federal funding for CDCs from 1966 to 1980 rose to over $500 million. In fact, the total charitable contributions to religious organizations amounted to $11.7 billion in 1974.

In 1990 charitable giving within the United States was estimated to be $100.5 billion. There were about 23,401 foundations with combined assets of $142.5 billion. That year, CDCs were given special set-aside funding as part of the 1990 Federal Housing Act. Additionally, in the 1980s HIV and AIDS became an increasing health epidemic in America and a number of faith-based groups responded with love and support. In 1990 MANNA was formed by the First Presbyterian Church of Philadelphia to lend resources and support to Americans living with AIDS as stigma and ignorance were standing in the way of caring for people in need. Each generation is faced with a health crisis or epidemic that thrusts charitable organizations into action. Missionaries traveling to Liberia treated those infected with the Ebola virus, stopping the outbreak from spreading and preventing further outbreaks. Doctors and missionaries traveling to South America and the Caribbean educated and aided populations most affected by the mosquito-borne Zika virus.

THE TWENTY-FIRST CENTURY

The shape of philanthropy forever changed in the United States around the beginning of the twenty-first century as the result of two families. Shadowing the generosity of the Carnegies and the Rockefellers, Bill Gates, the genius behind Microsoft, contributed $1 billion to the William H. Gates Foundation on his forty-third birthday in 1998. In December of the same year, he and his wife announced a $100 million gift to make vaccines for children more widely available. Furthermore, Warren Buffet, another one of the world's richest men, announced he would give $43.5 billion in Berkshire Hathaway stock to private foundations and charities.

More than a century after de Tocqueville's *Democracy in America* articulated his view on the role of associations in providing for the well-being of its citizens, it still holds true. Today, the nonprofit sector in the United States is impressively large and continuously growing. As of 2016 there are more than 1.5 million nonprofit organizations registered with the IRS. Nearly 70 percent of these organizations are public charities. In 2017, $410 billion was donated to charity. $127.37 billion was given to religion, representing 31 percent of the total. This percentage was down from 2016, 2015, and 2014. Giving to the subsectors of Human Services and Education have increased.

U.S. Trust and the Lilly Family School of Philanthropy released a study called "The 2016 U.S. Trust Study of High Net Worth Philanthropy." The study found that 91 percent of high net-worth households gave to charity in 2015, and more than 49 percent of those households gave to religious organizations. Sixty-three percent of those households gave to organizations that provide basic necessities to the people or communities they serve.

At this rate, it will be fascinating to see how many more charities will flower as new generations of people will come to shape and populate our modern society. The internet and other technologies have also presented new opportunities for philanthropy, with crowdfunding and text donations showing promise. The ALS Ice Bucket Challenge that began in 2014 demonstrated new potential for social media to encourage giving. Facebook users posted short videos of themselves pouring buckets of ice water over their heads and challenging their friends to follow suit in the name of awareness of Amyotrophic Lateral Sclerosis, also known as Lou Gehrig's disease. The campaign raised over $100 million. All of this information points to abundance, rather than scarcity. The challenge is to strategically plan your fundraising efforts.

Questions for Discussion and More Research

1. What does charitable giving in America mean for your organization?
2. Americans are willing to be generous if they believe in a cause. What religious beliefs drive their giving?
3. Wealthy individuals have driven many of the impactful advances in the nonprofit world. How do middle-income individuals change their communities?
4. What do economic and social trends say about the future of philanthropy for your organization?

Steps You Can Take Right Now

1. Subscribe to newsletters and magazines from thought leaders in the sector, such as "Philanthropy News

Digest," a daily news service from the Foundation Center; "The Chronicle of Philanthropy"; and publications from Lake Institute on Faith & Giving at the Lilly School of Philanthropy, Grantmakers for Effective Organizations, and the Institutional Religious Freedom Alliance.

2. Start or join a book club focused on faith and charity. Invite people with views and beliefs different from your own.

3. Keep a journal of your thoughts and prayers concerning generosity and gratitude.

4. Collaborate with nonprofit organizations—serve your community.

5. Form your own "kitchen cabinet" of advisors to bounce off ideas and connections to potential donors

Bibliography for Chapter 1

Arnsberger, Paul, Melissa Ludlum, Margaret Riley, and Mark Stanton. "A History of the Tax-Exempt Sector." The Internal Revenue Service. Winter 2008. https://www.irs.gov/pub/irs-soi/tehistory.pdf.

Fleishman, Joel L. *The Foundation: A Great American Secret: How Private Wealth Is Changing the World.* New York: PublicAffairs, 2009.

Salamon, Lester M. "America's Nonprofit Sector: A Primer." The Foundation Center. April 1999.

U.S. Department of Justice. Office of Justice Programs Fact Sheet. "Faith-Based Programs." November 2011. http://ojp.gov/newsroom/factsheets/ojpfs_faith-basedprog.html.

U.S. Trust and the Indiana University Lilly Family School of Philanthropy. "The 2016 U.S. Trust Study of High Net Worth Philanthropy: Charitable Practices of and Preferences of Wealthy Households." October 2016. https://www.ustrust.com/publish/content/application/pdf/GWMOL/USTp_ARMCGDN7_oct_2017.pdf.

Zunz, Oliver. *Philanthropy in America: A History.* Princeton, New Jersey: Princeton University Press, 2014.

Chapter Two

Many Are Called, But Few Are Chosen: Leadership with Impact

So, he shepherded them according to the integrity of his heart, and guided them by the skillfulness of his hands.

—Psalm 78:72 (NKJV)

BALANCING LEADERSHIP AND FAITH

Leaders of faith-based organizations have enormous responsibilities. The qualities that make a leader—authority and strength—may seem to contradict the humility associated with people of faith. These contradictions need to be acknowledged and embraced. The values that drive the mission of the organization can help you balance the competing expectations of staff, board, and other stakeholders. It is possible to be a strong leader while maintaining your humility and your spiritual integrity. In fact, without those qualities, leadership is a useless, even dangerous, thing.

"One life influencing another," says author and pastor John Maxwell. "This is the heart of leadership." A leader is someone capable of influencing the behavior of others. The actions you're taking may be admirable and worthwhile, inspiring or courageous, but if nobody else is involved, that's not leadership. As a wise person once phrased it: If you call yourself a leader and nobody's following you—then you're just taking a walk. Look behind you. Is there anybody there?

What qualities come to mind when you hear the word *leader*? You may think about strength, authority, or influence. It may involve shouting commands like a drill sergeant or, in Teddy Roosevelt's immortal phrase, speaking softly and carrying a big stick, but leadership requires the exertion of power over others. Whether the person wielding leadership possesses overtly authoritative characteristics or carries a smaller stick, leaders inevitably act from a position of power.

Now ask yourself what qualities come to mind when you hear the word *faith*. Are you picturing someone on his or her knees, asking for forgiveness from the Lord? Perhaps you yourself know the profound experience of submitting to the authority of a higher power. Faith can take many forms, but in order to be genuine, it definitely involves humility. No matter how ambitious or commanding you are, the authority that counts is the one that comes from above.

Can leaders have it both ways? Can they be both powerful *and* humble? Can they exert authority in the workplace without sacrificing the essential modesty of religious faith? The simple answer is yes, but the reality involves balancing oppositional demands and embracing contradictory impulses. This fascinating tension is what I'll explore in this chapter.

EMBRACING THE CONTRADICTIONS

You don't have to conceal your humility to be a strong leader, and you don't have to stifle your vision in order to be a person of faith. It's a balancing act, but it can be done.

Let's imagine you are a leader tackling an everyday issue. Picture this scenario: You recently became executive director of Elderchat, a (make-believe) organization dedicated to ensuring that homebound seniors in the community have companionship and someone to handle such minor inconveniences as broken appliances. Elderchat has a staff of three to organize year-round volunteer visits to retirement villages and other sites.

The problem is Doug. He's been with the organization since the beginning and still thinks it should be run the way it was always run. A closer look at the situation at Elderchat shows staff members typing information about volunteers and the seniors into Excel documents kept on separate computers. And that's when things are going well. Much of the time, no records are kept at all of visits or what services were provided.

One of your priorities is implementing a new CRM (customer relationship management) system to ensure continuity when a staff member departs, to engage volunteers as donors, and more. In fact, when you took the job you promised the board you would accomplish this goal in your first three months.

Doug's not into it. "We are already too busy," he announces, without even bothering to shut your office door. "We've tried things like this before, and they've never worked. What's wrong with our spreadsheets, anyway?"

As the new leader of this small but established organization, you are within your rights to insist that Doug must adopt the new system or pack his bags. This "my way or the highway" approach has been the default of bosses since the dawn of time. If Doug can't get with the program, there are plenty of people out there who could fill his shoes.

Before you rush into judgment, however, let me tell you more about Doug. When it comes to making a connection to seniors, he's truly gifted—empathetic and genuine, with seemingly inexhaustible patience. On more than one occasion he's ridden in an ambulance holding a client's hand on the way to the emergency room. Doug also has good relationships with the volunteers and other members of the team, and he's known a few of the board members for more than a decade.

My point isn't to tell you what to do about Doug, but rather to encourage you to keep your options open. Yes, you are accountable for results, but this is an organization that depends on healthy, trusting relationships. And the way you treat staff ought to mirror the caring way your staff treats clients.

What if you put Doug in charge of selecting the CRM and training his coworkers? That might make him feel more engaged in the process. Alternatively, you could shift resources around so that Doug can fully use his vital skill sets, and another team member can be paired with him for the data-entry tasks that he resents.

> "I believe in a *serving* leadership. You come to serve others, not to be served. In ministry, we view people as family. If they're hurting, I'm hurting."
>
> —THELMA HAGOOD, HR Director,
> First Baptist Church of Glenarden, Upper Marlboro Maryland

Finally, and most importantly, you can open up to Doug and discuss the issues with him, thereby sharing your deeply held belief in the mission of the organization. Tell him about what your grandmother went through after your grandfather died. Ask him for advice. Pray with him for a solution. A "my way or the highway" kind of leader might hear all these options and say you are showing weakness. But unless you are willing to be vulnerable, you might find yourself all alone at the top of a defunct organization.

With the right balance, you can act in the best interests of your cause and maintain your personal spiritual integrity.

FOUNDER/LEADERS

Founding a nonprofit is not for the fainthearted. Making the decision to lead a faith-based organization should be undertaken only after prayer and careful consideration, as well as consultation with trusted advisors. Nonprofit founders come from all walks of life. Perhaps you are a veteran at fundraising or service delivery with the desire to strike out on your own, or you may be a recent college graduate eager to prove an innovative new concept. Other founders come from the foundation or corporate world. Having made financial grants and gone through the due diligence required to assess nonprofits, these professionals have the perspective to identify unmet needs in the community.

Potential founders of faith-based nonprofits similarly emerge from any number of sectors, but there is one major difference. In addition to other relevant life experiences, these founders generally have ties to a church or denomination with spiritual values that underlie their determination to make a positive change for their community or world. Faith supports the decision to launch a new organization, the strategy for realizing positive outcomes, and everything from office staffing to office supplies.

Making up your mind about starting a new venture like this should not be done hastily. It is a personal process that should involve a great deal of prayer, heartfelt discussions with family and friends, and consultation with trusted advisors and mentors. Ultimately, the decision is between you and God, but a good litmus test is whether the prospective organization has a *mission* that stirs your soul. The next chapter will help you understand the importance of mission and get you started on crafting one of your own.

ELIMINATE CLOUDED PRIORITIES

King David is known today as one of the Great Leaders. He was a soldier, a poet, and a servant of God. He was also a sinner. David carried on an adulterous affair with Bathsheba and sent her husband, Uriah, to die in battle. In doing so, he made a bad thing worse. As has happened repeatedly with political and other leaders in modern times, the cover-up was worse than the crime.

One betrayal leads to another. The sin ripples outward. Among David's casualties was his nephew Joab, a field officer who led military campaigns against Syria, Ammon, and Edom. Joab carried out David's orders, but he paid a dear price—losing God's faith in him. As stated in Ezekiel 22:30: "So I sought for a man among them who would make a wall, and stand in the gap before Me on behalf of the land, that I should not destroy it; but I found no one."

Clearly, David put his own desires ahead of the needs of his people. In your workplace, bad decisions probably won't leave corpses on a battlefield, but nevertheless you should ask yourself often whether your motives are pure.

Leaders of nonprofits must identify deeply with the missions of their organizations. Whether it's rescuing strays, celebrating heritage, or teaching entrepreneurship, the mission takes precedence over the needs and priorities of the person in charge.

It's okay for a leader to have a large personality (a lot of leaders do, after all, and not just in the Bible). Looking good, dressing well, and speaking in a forceful manner are all things that can be harnessed to advance the mission of the organization. Being called on to advise powerful people in your community because of your work is a common perk. The problem comes when priorities get confused and the leader puts him or herself ahead of the organization he or she has been called upon to serve.

> "When I worked in the corporate world and someone came into my office with an issue, I would listen, then take out the policy manual and make a recommendation. Now that I work for a faith-based organization, my first step is to pray. I listen to hear their heart, not their head. The Holy Spirit guides me to help them resolve this issue." —THELMA HAGOOD

LEADERSHIP AND FISCAL RESPONSIBILITY

We all have heard and read about scandals in the nonprofit world. Leaders get caught "borrowing" from the organization's bank account for the purposes of home renovation. My blood boils when I read about these instances that, thank God, are the outliers and not the norm. What a betrayal of trust! Supporters are asked to donate their hard-earned money so one person can own and fly in a $24 million-dollar private jet. Lavish fundraisers sometimes do more for the caterers and party planners than for the cause. Nonprofit leaders being chauffeured in a Bentley or Rolls Royce? This is unacceptable. More recently we have seen a spate of sexual harassment charges and mass resignations in Christian-based organizations that have placed a laser light on leadership behavior.

Donor trust has been tested. Their faith has been shaken by a few people who've knowingly or unknowingly made bad decisions. The scandals taint not just the organization in question but also the entire sector, the very charitable impulse that drives our humility and humanity. Just as faith in the Lord holds our spiritual lives together, faith in the organization is necessary for its life and growth.

Those who lead faith-based nonprofits must be held to a higher standard of excellence. We trust them to be financially prudent, to live reasonably, and to make decisions based on the best interest of people (homelessness, hunger, aging, the environment, or whatever else their cause supports) that are in a vulnerable situation. Anything less than pure righteousness is likely to attract judgment. It's a very high standard but it comes with the turf.

As the leader of a nonprofit, you can't be perfect. You can't satisfy everybody, and you shouldn't expect to make it through the week without a small mistake—or the year without a big one. Your success or failure depends on how you retain your personal faith and recover from mistakes.

Bill Enright, Executive Director Emeritus, Lake Institute on Faith & Giving, says, "Unfortunately, stewardship really has nothing to do with fundraising. It's about being a faithful manager of the resources and possessions with which we have been blessed and we have been given. We corrupted the word 'stewardship,' and it became a synonym for 'fundraising.'"

I agree with Bill and add that integrity, good fiscal practices, and accountability are what's needed for a leader of a faith-based nonprofit.

"Let your light so shine before men, that they may see your good works, and glorify your Father which is in heaven."—Matthew 5:15–16

Questions for Discussion

1. Why do you want to be a leader?
2. If you were to *honestly* prioritize faith, power, money, and mission, in what order would they be?
3. How do you balance your professional and religious goals? Do you prioritize one over the other during certain periods of life?
4. Who are your most trusted advisors for your personal life? Are these people also the ones you trust discussing your professional goals?
5. Which biblical leader inspires you most? What are his or her flaws, and how did they overcome them?
6. When you reflect on a famous or historical leader, what inspires you most?
7. Which leaders from your own experience do you admire most? Why?
8. What is your Achilles' heel—the flaw or sin to which you're most susceptible? How will you work to mitigate this risk?

Steps You Can Take Right Now

1. Identify and recruit a few "accountability partners" outside of your organization whom you can trust to tell you the truth.
2. Revisit your organization's performance review procedure and make sure that there is a way for the leader to receive candid feedback.

3. Set expectations for the staff and/or volunteers who will be working to support the organization. Align those expectations with the mission as the foundation.

4. At the start of each week (or month, whatever works for you), sketch out a vision for what you want to achieve, and when the week is over, take it out and rate your own performance. If it helps keep you accountable, ask a trusted friend or mentor to join you in this exercise.

5. Think back to the last three decisions you made as a leader. Ask yourself how your faith and values were—or were not—reflected in those decisions.

6. From among the three decisions you considered in the previous step, which one least embodies your deeply held values? How can you make it right tomorrow? Can you seek forgiveness?

7. Find a biblical or spiritual passage that inspires you and copy it down into a notebook, longhand, word by word. Now read it aloud and listen to how the words sound in your ears. This is your leadership voice. Now use it!

Bibliography for Chapter 2

Bonbright, David, and Denver Frederick. *The Business of Giving with Denver Frederick*. January 28, 2016.

FaithSearch Partners. "Executive Onboarding Checklist for Faith-Based Non-profits: 9 Keys to Equipping New Leaders in Nonprofit Organizations with Faith-Based Missions." White paper PDF file.

Jackson, Barbara-Shae. "8 Church Scandals That May Have Challenged Your Faith." Atlanta Black Star, April 28, 2014.

Maxwell, John. *3 Things Successful People Do: The Road Map That Will Change Your Life*. Thomas Nelson, Harper Collins Leadership edition, 2016.

Tandon, Atul. "10 Steps for Success as a Nonprofit CEO." *The Chronicle of Philanthropy*, February 11, 2016.

Y Scouts. (https://yscouts.com/ "15 Outstanding Questions Leaders Ask Themselves Every Day." September 10, 2014. Accessed June 2017.

Chapter Three

The Business of
Your Faith-Based Organization:
Leading with the Mission

*For I know the plans I have for you, declares the Lord, plans for welfare
and not for evil, to give you a future and a hope.*
—Jeremiah 29:11 (ESV)

What do we do? Who we do it for? What is the impact? These are the three
critical questions a mission statement must answer. An important first
step is crafting a mission statement, the sentences that will tie your
operation to its purpose and meaning. The process of writing the
mission statement is almost as important as the words themselves.
Over time, organization leaders will want to check that the operations continue to harmonize with the mission. Asking the questions,
why we exist and what we believe relative to the work, sets the stage
for an accurate and powerful mission statement.

LIVING THE MISSION

A mission is more than a slogan or catchphrase. It is your organization's unique reason for existence and ideally a sacred calling. Slogans
can be clever or striking, but like other forms of marketing, they may
eventually go out of style. Missions are mostly evergreen. However, I
do recommend revisiting the mission to make sure you are on track
and to also revise it if necessary.

Consider the example of St. Paul's Episcopal Church in Pater-
son, New Jersey, which formed the St. Paul's Community Development Corporation in 1990 (see chapter 8 for more information about
community development corporations). The surrounding community

faced a number of economic and social challenges, and St. Paul's could not solve them all. The mission it set out for itself had to be ambitious and compelling on one hand, but also realistic and concrete on the other. Here is what they came up with:

> "The mission of St. Paul's Community Development Corporation is to serve as an agent of hope, partnering with others to provide needs-driven services that improve the quality of life and encourage greater self-sufficiency."

This framework is not just an abstract laundry line for hanging various programs. It is rooted in the theology of its church, which urges believers to be involved in the world we live in, while at the same time rising above it in hope and service. Growing out of this belief, the mission sets the stage for a range of interrelated services, including a food pantry, a men's shelter, a workforce development operation, housing development, and a program for young people that have been involved in the criminal justice system.

Another example worth considering is the Salvation Army, which began in Victorian England and now operates in 127 countries. Its mission statement reads:

> "The Salvation Army, an international movement, is an evangelical part of the universal Christian Church. Its message is based on the Bible. Its ministry is motivated by the love of God. Its mission is to preach the gospel of Jesus Christ and to meet human needs in His name without discrimination."

There is nothing in the mission statement about bell-ringing Santa Clauses requesting donations during the Christmas season, but this signature effort certainly fits, along with their music programs, prison rehabilitation, disaster relief, and much more. They are an international organization with the Bible as their foundation. The "without discrimination" aspect of their mission is not just rhetoric; it is backed up by a commitment to helping people regardless of race, gender, ethnicity, or sexual orientation.

On a more modest scale, Cresset Christian Academy in Durham, North Carolina, aims to ensure that its students develop a biblical worldview and stewards their spiritual growth. Rigorous academics are most definitely part of the program; nearly 100 percent of seniors pursue post-secondary education. Here is their mission statement:

> "Our mission is to cultivate the HEART of each student—
> to educate, to nurture, and to help shape their character
> in a Christ-centered environment grounded in the Truth
> of God's Word."

Student achievement is not mentioned, but *education* and *character* through a Christ-centered environment leads directly to this outcome.

SEEKING A MISSION

Mission statements provide direction for the organization, and the very process of writing one can help you clarify your purpose. Over time, a mission statement can serve as a yardstick to help you determine whether potential new programs are appropriate or whether existing programs have drifted away from their original intent. A good mission statement can rally support from within the organization as well as from outside parties such as donors and the media. Programs and community needs may fluctuate over time, and a mission statement should be flexible enough to accommodate change.

The process of creating a mission statement is nearly as important as the words themselves. This isn't a solitary job between you and your diary but rather the first critical opportunity to engage stakeholders. A group brainstorm or a series of two- or three-person meetings should include all or most of the following:

- Current or potential board members
- Staff and volunteers

- Leaders of the denomination with which the organization is affiliated

- Local elected officials

- People who will be served by the organization

These stakeholders should all be allowed to share their voice, their story, and their faith. Not all suggestions, no matter how strongly voiced, will end up in the final statement, but participants should come away feeling that they have been listened to. You may want to enlist a consultant to manage the process and to ensure objectivity—after all, you may be too close to your "baby" to integrate constructive suggestions.

At the end of this process, you should have landed on a statement that can be the lodestar for your organization. If done right, it won't have been easy. There will have been disagreements, well-intentioned critiques, and digressions on everything from finance to scripture. You may even have to part ways with someone who just can't get with the consensus. But if you think writing a mission statement was difficult, you should consider one thing: Nonprofits are group efforts, and every single day of your organization's existence will demand negotiations and compromises. You ain't seen nothing yet!

Building on the Mission— Without Drifting Away

By itself, the mission statement doesn't do anything to help people or communities. The *work* of the faith-based nonprofit is what people will know you by. The mission is that first gust of wind, pushing you in the right direction.

It would be nice if the next steps came in sequence, one after the other, but it's more likely that you'll be working on multiple objectives at once—recruiting the board, raising capital, forming partnerships. These endeavors are covered in subsequent chapters, and many of them can be so exhilarating that you and your staff will be swept away by all the possibilities. That's where the mission plays a crucial role, reminding you why you're doing this, what your calling is, and who you are.

Mission drift, also called mission creep, happens when an organization chases a shiny object and ends up becoming something that contradicts the original intent. For example, if your mission calls upon you to improve the health and nutrition of your community, a big grant from a fast-food corporation might seem attractive, but such a partnership could jeopardize the whole organization, alienating board members and other funders. Along the same lines, if the environment is your primary concern, you should beware of taking advantage of too many opportunities to fly around the country for conferences and speaking engagements. Jet planes use a lot of fossil fuel.

The same stakeholders who helped you craft the mission statement can be trusted advisors and truth-tellers to remind you of the sincere and idealistic conversations that took place at the genesis of the organization. The flow chart shows how the mission and other critical parts of your organization should flow.

And of course, prayer and Bible study can help you set or correct your course like nothing else.

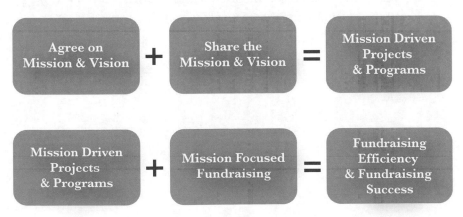

Questions for Discussion

1. What's the difference between the mission statements of a nonprofit organization and a corporation?

2. What could go wrong with a mission statement that is too general—or too specific?

3. What sources could you draw inspiration from as you draft a mission statement?

4. How do you ensure that you stay on track with the mission?

5. How do you handle course correction?

6. How would you rate the mission statements cited in this chapter against the three question criteria?

Steps You Can Take Right Now

1. Create a "Vision Board" with your personal and professional ambitions. See http://miriamnicolehuffman.com/christian-entrepreneurs-vision-boards-law-attraction for more information on this exercise.

2. Keep a journal with your favorite quotations—from the Bible and other sources.

3. Research the mission statements and histories of nonprofits both in your sector and beyond.

4. Interview the founder of a nonprofit you admire, and find out how its mission statement arose.

Bibliography for Chapter 3

"40 Nonprofit Vision Statements." Impacts. Accessed April 13, 2017.

Koenig, Marc. "Nonprofit Mission Statements—Good and Bad Examples." Nonprofit Hub. Accessed June 2016.

Litton, Matt. "A Call for the Christian Imagination: How to Bridge the Glaring Gap between This Hard Life and the Kingdom Reality." *RELEVANT* magazine, January 2013.

Rodman, Dr. Jeffrey E. "A Mission Statement, Vision Statement, and a Statement of Faith are Essential Components of Your Strategic Plan!" *The Christian Post*, April 2010.

Seattle Pacific University. "Explore Your Calling." Accessed July 2016. http://spu.edu/administration/center-career-calling/explore-your-calling

Chapter 4

Wisdom in a Multitude of Counselors: Building a Board

Where there is no counsel, the people fall;
But in the multitude of counselors there is safety.

—Proverbs 11:14 (NKJV)

A STRONG FOUNDATION

The board of directors of a nonprofit is also akin to a building's foundation. It needs to be sturdy and well thought out. That is why building a board matters most at the birth of the organization, but governance remains a primary concern throughout its existence. While harmony among board members and with the executive staff is important, diverse backgrounds and opinions can serve as a wellspring for creativity and innovation. Every board member has an important part to play, and every board member should be obligated to financially support the mission. One hundred percent financial-board participation is a MUST.

The success of your organization rests on its board of directors. These people are passionate volunteer leaders and engaged mentors who join the team equipped not only with Jesus's good will but also tangible and intangible resources to ensure growth and success. The board does not manage everyday operations; instead they make their wisdom, skills, and contacts available to the staff so that they can do their jobs better. By taking their governance role seriously, they assure the staff, donors, and other stakeholders that the organization has the credibility and wherewithal to fulfill its mission.

The board helps the organization to make the most of a good situation and helps it to mitigate the damage in the event of a crisis. During high points, low points, and everything in between, trusting, productive relationships are needed among board members and with the executive leaders. Without this atmosphere of trust, even a shared faith won't get you very far.

> "Serving on a nonprofit board is a privilege and an opportunity to be involved in something significant."
>
> —ELMIRA BAYRASLI, *Forbes*

In my experience, more often than not, when an organization checks its web analytics to see which pages have the most visits, it's the "About Us" page that lists the board of directors. When people want to find out about you, they look to see who your champions are, who has enough faith in you to put their names out there where everyone can see it.

Building a strong board for your nonprofit organization is one of the most important and fundamental things you can do because without it, all your well-intended hard work can, and will, eventually crumble. One of my most treasured mentors, Jerry Panas, would often say: "Choose your board as if the life of the organization depends on it . . . and it does!" He also said, "Some nonprofits don't get the board they need, they get the board they deserve." This latter statement usually creates a lot of tension when I am training groups of nonprofit leaders, but it gets people thinking about the necessary and vital due diligence of board recruitment.

GOVERNANCE IN ACTION

Since publishing an earlier book, *7 Fatal Flaws of Nonprofit Boards and How to Fix Them,* I have had the opportunity to meet hundreds of executive directors and board members. Many of the same issues come up again and again. One of them is a disconnect regarding what is expected of the board. With clear communication of mutual expectations, misunderstandings can be cleared up before problems worsen.

Board members are volunteers. They literally do this out of the goodness of their hearts. They donate their time. They donate their money. When organizational leaders come to me with concerns about board members who miss meetings, fail to return phone calls, or who—at the other end of the spectrum—meddle in the day-to-day operations, I remind them that these people are performing an essential service without any compensation.

The highly esteemed American nonprofit organization Board-Source, founded in 1988, gives a brief overview of board responsibilities in a nonprofit setting:

"Fiduciary duty requires board members to stay objective, unselfish, responsible, honest, trustworthy, and efficient. Board members, as stewards of public trust, must always act for the good of the organization, rather than for the benefit of themselves. They need to exercise reasonable care in all decision making, without placing the organization under unnecessary risk."

—BOARDSOURCE

Making sure that the nonprofit is complying with laws and regulations is just the beginning. Full participation in the organization's strategic plan and collaborating with the executive team on how to strategically use resources are constant demands. Board members can help the cause by serving as a sounding board, a doubting Thomas, or a devil's advocate.

It's good to take a look at the people around the table. Everyone plays an important role. The board chair (sometimes called the chairman) is elected by the board to lead the board for a certain term (often two or three years). He or she runs the meetings and is the primary liaison between the board and the executive team. At events such as galas or ribbon cutting ceremonies, the chair is usually expected to say a few words or to lead a prayer.

The board also has a treasurer who monitors the finances and participates extensively in the aspects of the strategic plan that involve dollars and cents—the budget, fundraising projections, and major multiyear outlays of cash. It is useful but not necessary for this person to have a banking or accounting background.

The secretary records minutes at each board meeting and circulates them before the next meeting so that the board can approve them. (This is usually the first item of business at each meeting.) Minutes don't have to be extensive or elaborate, but they should cover all the major decisions made. On rare occasions, such as lawsuits or IRS investigations, these documents have pivotal importance, and the responsibility should be taken very seriously.

The remaining members of the board are considered "at large," and they may head up committees or task forces as necessary. A governance committee, concerning the functions of the board itself and recruiting new members, is always advisable, as is a finance committee (which may or may not include fundraising) and a program committee. The head of each committee should give a brief report at each board meeting.

Board meetings aren't just about reports. They should be occasions for debate, discussion, and brainstorming. Fellowship among board members arises from free and candid dialogue. At the same time, the agenda should be tight and focused so that people with busy schedules don't feel like their time is being wasted. After all, they aren't getting paid to sit there.

A Diverse Team

If you are a founder, it may seem tempting and easy to simply recruit friends and loved ones to join your board. After all, these are the people who believe in you and who care the most about the success of your organization. This maneuver may seem like a recipe for harmony, but the outcome is more often conflict and dysfunction. Stocking the board with personal relations is a surefire way to sabotage your nonprofit.

You want a diverse group of people who bring fresh and varied perspectives to the table. Furthermore, if worse comes to worst and the board (your family and friends) must get rid of the organization's CEO (you), relationships will dissolve, and so will the organization.

Board members nourish an organization with a variety of different perspectives and kinds of expertise. Think of a potluck of skilled professionals bringing their A game to the table. Recruit people with backgrounds in law, finance, marketing, fundraising, labor, writing, public speaking, and the like. Identify people of different ethnicities, ages, and genders. However, do not try to diversify just to fit a demographic role. Balance the scales with type A and type B individuals. Then identify and understand what your specific nonprofit needs to flourish, and find the best people who will be just as passionate about the project. It is not enough to find the "perfect" person who excels at their job. Gather together individuals who will wholeheartedly accept the mission and the challenges they may face.

If you are the executive director (sometimes called the CEO) of the organization, you will want to develop a trusting and candid relationship with each board member. Recognize the balance of power that will come into play, and set clear guidelines about each member's role in the organization. Know that the board must not micromanage. The board's job is to advise the CEO in the direction of the nonprofit's prosperity and success. It is there to support, encourage, and inspire greatness.

THE BOARD'S PHILANTHROPIC RESPONSIBILITIES

Some boards have a "give or get" policy. I recommend give *and* get. Nonprofits require a significant amount of money in order to accomplish the goals they set for themselves. To achieve their missions, they need funding. The "give *and* get" policy allows for the mutually beneficial relationship between the board and the organization to flower into fruition. If a board member is serious about the organization, then they should be just as passionate as its founder. Moreover, if the board is as serious about the organization's success, they will be willing to financially contribute. Board members should be obligated to make a personally meaningful financial contribution to the organization. In fact, there should be a minimum gift contribution required from each member to add to the nonprofit's annual operating fund.

The minimum fee can be set commensurate to the board's average personal budget. Nowadays, most foundations ask if a nonprofit organization's board has a "100 percent giving" policy. If your organization cannot answer that question truthfully, then the chances of being considered by that foundation becomes significantly slimmer. This exhibits the importance of demonstrating to the funding community that board members generously support their organization.

> **TIP:** *Believe in the psychology of abundance, not scarcity!*

You've explored developing the groundwork of your nonprofit organization by establishing an active, diverse, and informed board of directors. Although this list from my book *7 Fatal Flaws of Nonprofit Boards and How to Fix Them* is not an exhaustive list, it is an attempt to prioritize some first steps in identifying hot spots and offer a few solutions.

SEVEN FATAL FLAWS OF NONPROFIT BOARDS

Fatal Flaw #1: Lack of Understanding Regarding Roles and Responsibilities

People often agree to serve on nonprofit boards without having a clear understanding of the work and financial commitment expected of them. Consequently, they are blindsided when they are asked to contribute a significant amount of time and money to the organization. Nonprofit organizations (NPOs) that are inexperienced with board functioning often give limited information to a prospective board member, assuming the person knows what it means to join the board. Some NPOs also fear that setting expectations will scare away prospective board members, so they wait until the person is involved before asking for money and time. All too often buyer's remorse sets in for both parties, resulting in an unsatisfactory board experience for the member and the NPO. The complaints that inevitably ensue negatively affect the progress of the organization. An NPO needs ambassadors and advocates, not uninformed, disgruntled current and former board members.

How to Fix This Flaw

Write job descriptions for board members and have the board approve them. Spell out all expectations and requirements for prospective and current board members, and be clear about the financial needs of the organization. Have every board member review and sign a letter of board agreement annually.

Fatal Flaw #2: Accepting Board Members Who Serve in Name Only

Having celebrity and other high-profile personalities on an NPO's board roster is meaningless if they never attend meetings or contribute financially in a substantive manner. Furthermore, their lack of involvement will have a negative impact on other board members. The objective all NPOs should have for their boards is the achievement of their mission through full financial and personal participation. If the organization falls short of its goals because of a lack of funds, then it is suffering from a mission deficit as well as a fiscal deficit because the board is not supporting the budget it has approved.

How to Fix This Flaw

Find other ways to use high-profile people if they cannot fully participate as board members. Giving them a special award at an event—if they have done something to deserve it and agree to be present to accept it—is one way to capitalize on their appeal and bring them closer to your organization.

Fatal Flaw #3: No Board Training or Orientation

Far too many NPOs skip this important process. During board audits members are often asked if they were given a formal orientation to their responsibilities and a review of the organization's guidelines, policies, and strategic plan. Too often the answer is no, which is unfortunate because an informed board member is a strong board member. NPOs should not forgo training and orientation sessions because they believe board members are too busy to attend. Good board members will make the time.

How to Fix This Flaw

Compile a board book that includes executive summaries of the NPO's strategic plan, full bylaws, board members' job descriptions, organizational chart, etc. Hold an orientation session with appropriate staff and new board members. If you have never held an orientation, include all board members. Make sure the training session is well-organized and efficient.

Fatal Flaw #4: No Active Board Committees

A board without active committees is usually a weak board. Without such a structure, NPOs (no matter how small) are not taking full advantage of the board's talents. Without committees leading the way on important NPO matters such as cultivating and recruiting new board members (nominating committee), overseeing fundraising plans (development committee), and ensuring the organization's fiscal health (finance committee), the board will not be as strong as it could be and the work will fall to the same few people, leading to burnout and dysfunction.

How to Fix This Flaw

Create a nominating committee to recruit new board members, a development committee to review all fundraising efforts, and a finance committee to assist in overseeing the financial aspects of the NPO. Remember that individuals who are subject-matter experts but not board members can also serve on selected committees. Don't overlook opportunities to engage their expertise.

Fatal Flaw #5: Tolerating Less Than Excellent Leadership

A weak leader is a death knell for a successful board. Charisma doesn't automatically translate into sound leadership, and the lack of it doesn't either. A board chairman who does not lead by example in support of the organization is inappropriate. Some organizations accept weak board chairmen because no one else was interested. Imagine the signal that sends to everyone in the organization, especially if that person is ineffective. A board chairman's ability to earn respect from others through good leadership, conduct well-run meetings, and practice an inclusive leadership style will have a positive impact on the NPO.

How to Fix This Flaw

Aggressively recruit good leaders as if the life of the organization depends on it—and it does. Create an advisory committee for well-meaning people who want to be involved but lack the capacity to lead the organization. Stop accepting less than the organization needs and deserves.

Fatal Flaw #6: A Board That Is Not the Right Size or Composition

Boards can be too large and unwieldy or too small and overburdened. If a board is not the right size, organizational instability can occur. Furthermore, when a board lacks diversity and the right mix of expertise, the organization deprives itself of the energy and resources to prosper. Not enough thought is given to questions such as: Do we need more board members? Fewer members? Do we have the right people? Many experts say the size of a board depends on the size of the organization and its budget. And while we're on the subject of board size, don't forget to consider term limits for board members. Too often ineffective board members are allowed to remain because of longevity or for political reasons, which does not help the organization move forward.

How to Fix This Flaw

Give the nominating committee the job of analyzing the board's size and composition. Hire an outside consultant to conduct a board audit and make objective recommendations about size and composition. Recognizing the problem is the first step toward a strategic solution.

Fatal Flaw #7: A Board That Relies Solely on Staff for Fundraising

"Isn't that what we hired the development director to do?" All too often, that is how board members respond when they are asked to make a generous contribution to the organization. Instead, board members should be working in partnership with the development staff to make sure the organization is financially vibrant and viable. Development teams that take sole responsibility for fundraising efforts hinder the participation and growth of the organization's board. Boards that rely on staff for fundraising are dysfunctional.

How to Fix This Flaw

Strong boards equal strong fundraising. Therefore, provide the framework for a fundraising partnership by training board members and creating a sound fundraising plan. Define roles and responsibilities for staff and the board and hold people accountable for adhering to them. Such board/staff partnerships have proven highly successful for organizations that have adopted this strategic direction.

*   *   *

In conclusion, having a well-planned, diverse board makes the difference between a good nonprofit and a great one. To have a board that embraces its leadership role fully and knows the difference between micromanaging and governing only ensures the organization's road to success. Just as commitment is imperative in any relationship, so it goes for a nonprofit's board and its members.

Questions for Discussion

1. How will you recognize a good potential board member when you see one?

2. Capacity to make a financial donation is one trait that might make a potential board member attractive. What else do you look for?

3. What are some intangible qualities you would look for in a board member? (For example, emotional intelligence or religious faith.)

4. How do you make yourself and your organization attractive to potential board members?

Steps You Can Take Right Now

1. Draw up a list of fantasy board members. This is an imaginary board, so you can include fictional characters or people who are no longer with us, such as Harriet Tubman.

2. Ask a friend if you could conduct a mock board interview with them. Have the friend come up with hard questions to ask you about your organization.

3. Develop a matrix of qualities, specific skills, age, gender, race/ethnicity, etc. of the current board.

4. Create a recruitment strategy template for potential board members.

5. Research contracts drawn up between nonprofits and board members and think of which clauses you might want to include in yours.

Bibliography for Chapter 4

Bayrasli, Elmira. "Building Successful Non-Profit Boards." *Forbes*, June 2011. http://www.forbes.com/sites/elmirabayrasli/2011/06/06/building-successful -non-profit-boards/#329b5ce87599

Hall, Peter Dobkin. *A History of Nonprofit Boards in the United States.* BoardSource, 2003. http://greatkreations.com/library/nonprofBOD_US.pdf

Mission Increase Foundation. "Emerging Trends in Nonprofit Board Growth: Exploring Common Myths Regarding Small and Midsize Christian Nonprofits and Their Boards." 2010. https://www.missionincrease.org/media/2010%20MIF%20Board%20Survey.pdf

National Council of Nonprofits. "Finding the Right Board Members for your Nonprofit." Access date: November 2017. https://www.councilofnonprofits.org/tools-resources/finding-the-right -board-members-your-nonprofit

Stanley, Debbi. "Building a Strong Board in 6 Easy Steps." NP Engage. November 8, 2012. http://npengage.com/nonprofit-fundraising/building-strong-board-6-easy -steps/

Taylor, Nathaniel. "Board Governance and Special Rules for Faith-Based Nonprofits." Access date: February 17, 2014. http://www.sos.wa.gov/_assets/charities/2014%20Faith-Based%20Workshop. pdf

Chapter 5

The Decent and In-Order Factor: Getting the Basics Right

Let all things be done decently and in order.

—Corinthians 14:40 (NKJV)

INSTANT EFFICIENCY

For-profit corporations make it a point to operate with efficiency, innovation, and strategy. Nonprofits need to do the same. The measures you put in place early on will help steer your organization through difficult times and beyond the goals you set. Technological tools can help you to get organized and stay on track, and many of these applications are affordable and simple to master. In conjunction with technology, consultants may be useful to ensure that you are keeping pace with best practices. This will save you from potentially expensive problem solving and "fixes" down the line.

I think nonprofits have an undeserved reputation for inefficiency. In the US economic system, where profits are most often regarded as the ultimate value, the very term *nonprofit* can conjure images of long lunch breaks, technological backwardness, and leaders who are all heart and no head. This is nonsense. In my experience, there is every bit as much innovation and entrepreneurship in the nonprofit sector as there is in the business world. Some of the savviest leaders I know lead faith-based nonprofits.

In fact, there are concrete similarities between the for-profit corporate world and the nonprofit sector:

CORPORATIONS	NONPROFIT FAITH-BASED ORGANIZATIONS
Mission=Corporate Profits	Mission=Changed Lives
Sources of Money: Capitalization, Sales	Sources of Money: Fundraising, Earned Income
Customer-Centered	Donor-Centered
Vision	Vision
Core Values	Core Values
Engaged Board	Engaged Board
Strong Leader	Strong Leader
Know Customers	Know Donors
Marketing/Branding	Marketing/Branding
Strategic Plan	Strategic Plan
Products	Programs
Talented Employees (bonus incentives)	Talented Staff (passion for the mission)
Sound Financials	Sound Financials
Key Performance indicators	Evaluation

As a nonprofit leader, you have the opportunity to prove the doubters wrong. A wide range of tools are available for helping nonprofits manage everything from budgeting to banking, from marketing to membership. These tools are affordable, adaptable, and easy to use—even if your technical know-how is limited.

Implementing systems as soon as possible after launching a nonprofit will help you stay on top of all the little details as you expand. In the beginning, it may seem simpler to balance your checkbook by hand. You may be tempted to use one combined account for your personal finances and those of the organization. You'll sort it out later, you tell yourself. This is a recipe for disaster. Your good intentions may be paving the road to a painful audit. This chapter reviews some of the most reliable tools and strategies for building efficiency into your organization. So, let's start at the very beginning of setting up your faith-based nonprofit. If your nonprofit is already established you might review the following steps to make sure nothing was missed.

Dollars and Sense: Starting from Scratch

Your neighborhood bank probably offers accounts for nonprofits. In order to set one up, you need a Taxpayer Identification Number (TIN; sometimes called an Employer Identification Number or EIN). You can apply for this number through your financial advisor, or you can do it yourself on the IRS website and get instant approval.

You don't need an accountant or lawyer to file for nonprofit status. The IRS website has all the information you need. Remember that it may take six months or longer to get your approval, but you can legally still accept donations while approval is pending. (Some foundations and individuals may prefer to wait until you are "official.")

The bank's online account system may suffice for getting your financial house in order, or you may opt for one of the many online systems, most of which can be updated via smartphone apps. Quicken and QuickBooks, both products offered by Intuit, are two of the most popular. In general, Quicken is more suited to small organizations, which "graduate" to QuickBooks as they grow. Either one will be your friend when tax time comes around.

The IRS requires nonprofits to record donations before depositing them. Furthermore, contributions must be designated according to the donor's wishes—restricted to a certain program or unrestricted, that is, to be used for whatever purpose the nonprofit deems appropriate.

In order to comply with this requirement, your organization needs a customer-relationship management (CRM) tool. This is what you use to keep track of donors, volunteers, and other stakeholders, including the clients of your organization. For nonprofits, Blackbaud and Salesforce are two of the best-known companies in this space, but smaller outfits like EveryAction and Kindful are also worth considering. No matter which you choose, it will be far superior to maintaining an Excel spreadsheet.

> **TIP:** *Be sure that your CRM integrates with your financial software, so that you don't have to enter data in more than one system. Customer service will help you sync your accounts.*

Although CRM systems are designed to be operated by non-experts, it may be advisable to hire a consultant to customize the system to your organization and assist with matters that go beyond what customer service can provide. See the chapter on consultants for more on this topic.

> **TIP:** *A college intern who is studying IT could be very helpful to you in setting this system up as well. You can be very resourceful in getting help with your CRM setup.*

A CRM system is only as good as the data that is entered. Inconsistency is the enemy here, so you may want to designate one person—or a certain amount of time each week—for CRM maintenance. Discipline in this area today will be amply rewarded tomorrow. You will have an automatic "institutional memory" to help you recall a volunteer or foundation supporter even if staff members leave the organization—or if an occasional name or fact happens to escape you for the moment. Additionally, CRM systems are also helpful when doing marketing or event outreach and tracking patterns of giving and how much particular donors give over the course of a year or their relationship with the organization.

PROGRAM METRICS

As with financial tools, a range of programs and software applications exist for tracking progress toward program goals. Many nonprofits use "dashboards," which collect and present progress on key performance indicators (KPIs) at a glance. This tool can unite staff and board around agreed-upon goals. But first the decision must be made about what to measure and how to measure it.

It's important to take a step back and really look at this issue. Some readers might say, "I didn't get into this line of work so I could stare at a readout all day. I want to help people. That's what Jesus calls me to do." Yet a culture of data goes hand in hand with having a loving, worshipful approach to delivering services. Whether your nonprofit is focused on education, the environment, or any number of causes, it is vital to establish the objective measures of program performance.

This is not to say that *all* results can be measured. The smile on the face of a sick child or the warmth of a rescued dog on a cold winter night can never be reduced to a data point. However, your board and supporters will demand objective results as well as heart-warming stories. Foundations in particular are increasingly focused on the metrics to justify their investments.

Deciding on a method, program, or tool to evaluate program success is a vital step for your organization, so the entire board should be involved in this process. A faith-based nonprofit will have special concerns as this decision is made. Here are some examples:

- How are the program outcomes compatible with our values?

- If the organization is devoted to improving government policies, how far are we willing to go to achieve our aims? (See section on nonprofits and advocacy below.)

- To the extent that the organization pays vendors or purchases supplies, how important is it that our partners reflect your values?

- If the organization is devoted to helping people from other countries, how does it decide which geographical areas to serve?

> **TIP:** *Convene a task force to research possible means of measuring impact, and select two or three choices for presentation to the board. The outcome of the presentation should be a decision on a specific system.*

Underlying all these questions is a big question that goes back to the earlier discussions of the organization's mission and its strategic plan. Any allocation of funds or time implies a conviction that one activity is more important than the infinite number of other activities to which that resource could have gone. What is the yardstick for making those decisions?

COURSE CORRECTION

Back in the day when people used pencils, there was a popular saying when referring to mistakes: "That's why we have erasers." Well, we don't use pencils anymore, but we are still making mistakes. We call it course correction. It is perfectly fine to "course correct" when an organizational system, or culture, is feeding off something and going in the wrong direction.

My advice is to address the issue as soon as possible. Bring the issue to the board and have this great group of people help you solve the problem. Since solving the problem may include an expense, the board should be helpful in either providing pro bono services or agreeing to raise the money required (see chapter 4 on boards).

KEEPING YOUR NONPROFIT STATUS

Among the easiest and most important tasks you face is maintaining your nonprofit status. (Just because it's easy doesn't mean you should put it off!) For the purposes of this chapter we will assume that you are a 501(c)(3) public charity. If you are a private foundation or other type of nonprofit you should look into your yearly requirements, as they may be different; a good place to start would be the IRS website.

Most public charities are required to file a Form 990 annual return along with a Schedule A with the IRS to satisfy federal law requirements. Some organizations (such as churches) are exempt from this filing requirement yet file annual returns anyway because they wish to be transparent regarding their finances and operations. Consult with your attorney tax advisor on this issue. The IRS has a toll-free number to answer questions from tax-exempt organizations: (877) 829-5500. There may also be pro bono attorneys willing to assist you.

If your organization's tax year ends on December 31, your annual returns must be filed by May 15. If May 15 falls on a Saturday, Sunday, or federal holiday, your annual return is due on the following business day. If your organization has a different date for the ending of its tax year you can find out your due date by visiting the following table of return due dates provided by the IRS: https://www.irs.gov/charities-non-profits/return-due-dates-for-exempt-organizations-annual-return. You should always make sure to file your return on time or you may be subject to penalties. Additionally, you will automatically lose your tax exemption if you do not file a return for three consecutive years.

NONPROFITS AND ADVOCACY VERSUS LOBBYING

Let's now discuss some of the laws pertaining to nonprofit advocacy. Your nonprofit organization is allowed to engage in a wide variety of advocacy activities, some of which you may be engaged in without any limitation. For example, after a law has passed you may look to shape a particular bill by being involved in the process of creating regulatory rulemakings and regulations. You may engage in litigation efforts, such as lawsuits that challenge the lawfulness of existing statutes and laws. You can create clinics that inform people about what the law is and their legal rights, educate legislators about the issues facing the people or community your faith-based organization works with, and educate the people you work with about the legislative process. You can also assist with voter registration, research issues facing your community, and create a report and organize a rally about the issues your nonprofit works on. An important tool for many nonprofits is community organizing and mobilizing the community to create change.

Public charities may engage in a limited amount of lobbying. The lobbying laws are different for organizations other than 501(c)(3) public charities. For more information on laws for other types of nonprofits, visit the IRS or Alliance for Justice websites.

When nonprofit organizations advocate on their own behalf, they seek to affect some aspect of society, whether they appeal to individuals about their behavior, employers about their rules, or the government about its laws. Lobbying refers specifically to advocacy efforts that attempt to influence legislation.

Seeking legislation germane to the common business interest is a permissible means of attaining a business league's exempt purposes. Thus, an Internal Revenue Code (IRC) section 501(c)(6) business league may further its exempt purposes by lobbying as its sole activity without jeopardizing its exempt status. However, a section 501(c)(6) organization that engages in lobbying may be required either to notify its members about the percentage of dues that are used for lobbying activities or to pay a proxy tax.

You are probably now wondering what counts as lobbying. Lobbying can be defined as communications intended to influence specific legislation. There are two kinds of lobbying: direct and grassroots. Direct lobbying occurs when a communication is made to a legislator, an employee of a legislative body, or any other government employee who may participate in the formulation of legislation. The communication must reference a specific piece of legislation and express a view on it. For example, if the director of your organization called a senator and asked her to vote in favor of a bill that the senator would be voting on the following week, this would constitute direct lobbying. On the other hand, if the director asked the senator to have lunch to discuss your organization's homeless shelter and ask her to be the keynote speaker at a benefit because of her past work with homeless shelters in the area, that would not be direct lobbying.

Grassroots lobbying occurs when your organization encourages people other than your organization's members to contact their legislators. For it to be grassroots lobbying your organization must also refer to specific legislation, reflect a view on it, and encourage the recipient to take action. If your organization were to mail postcards to everyone in a zip code about the bill being voted on the following week, this would not be grassroots lobbying unless the postcards also asked the recipients to ask the senator to vote yes on the bill. There is a separate cap for grassroots lobbying, which may only be 25 percent of your organization's total lobbying expenditures. Organizations who exceed the lobbying limit under the 501(h) tests often do so with their grassroots lobbying.

A 501(c)(3) organization may not engage in partisan political activity and thus cannot support or oppose a candidate for office, be it a local, state, or national election. This does not mean that all election-related activity is banned for your organization. You simply may not engage in *partisan* activity such as asking people to vote for a certain candidate, state that your organization supports a particular political party, or have your organization make a contribution to a particular candidate. You may still assist in voter registration efforts, provide information to all candidates about issues your organization is involved in, and host a nonpartisan candidate forum where all the candidates are invited to attend.

In addition to federal law there may be state law requirements regarding your lobbying and electoral activities at the state or local level. For example, you may need to report your lobbying to your state each year. For more information about requirements in your state you should look at your Secretary of State's website.

With all of these concerns about nonprofit activity, how can your nonprofit be assured of keeping its tax-exempt status and not become subject to additional taxes? There are a number of things your faith-based organization should keep in mind when it comes to your fiduciary responsibilities.

One basic but important step is to comply with all of the relevant filing requirements in a timely manner and follow all laws. If there is something you are unsure about make sure to get additional information from a reputable party, such as the IRS or an attorney or accountant knowledgeable about such matters. Even if you disagree with a law or reporting requirement you must comply with it. The best way to handle disagreement with a law is to comply with it but register your disagreement with the legislator(s) who can take action on that law. Should the IRS or Congress question you about anything related to your nonprofit, respond to the inquiry in a prompt and accurate manner.

EXAMPLES OF LOBBYING ORGANIZATIONS:

ACLU   American Civil Liberties Union – Visit their section on issues before Congress that the ACLU is following and lobbying on.

ALDF   Animal Legal Defense Fund

ADL   Anti-Defamation League fights anti-Semitism

AERF   Atlas Economic Research Foundation

CCFR   California Campaign Finance Reform – A group trying to limit the influence of political campaign donors

CC   Common Cause – Citizens working to end special-interest politics and reform government ethics

CF   Commonwealth Fund – A group with a range of programs aimed at advancing better medical care in the United States

FOE   Friends of the Earth U.S. – Campaigns on issues including climate change, pollution, nuclear technology, genetic engineering, deforestation, pesticides, food and agriculture and economic policy. It is a founding member of Friends of the Earth International, the world's largest grassroots environmental network.

HPLI   Health Policy Leadership Institute – Aims to train US doctors and medical students in political action and advocacy

NRA   National Rifle Association – Visit the NRA's Institute for Legislative Action for an example of a highly organized lobbying effort. While I fundamentally disagree with many of NRA's policies, their lobbying tactics are something worth analyzing.

PACS   Political Action Committees – A list from Yahoo! of a type of organization in the United States directly aimed at promoting specific interests by supporting or opposing candidates in elections

TVC   Traditional Values Coalition

Questions for Discussion

1. What are some stories you've heard about nonprofits that made financial or legal mistakes? How could they have been avoided?

2. What are some other potential problems an organization could run into if it doesn't have its house in order?

3. Who is responsible for the financial, legal, and programmatic systems in your organization? Who supports that person?

4. One way to defray expenses for technology is to share resources with another organization. How could you find partners like this?

5. How can we ensure that our nonprofit status is protected?

Steps You Can Take Right Now

1. Interview an established nonprofit leader about the systems he or she has in place.

2. Accountants and other advisors will often provide free consultations. Make an appointment and find out what peer organizations do—and learn about mistakes to avoid.

3. Take a course online (see Lynda.com) or at a community college to brush up on your technology, accounting, non-profit management, or CRM skills.

4. Explore whether a local college can connect you to talented, tech-savvy students looking for volunteer experience. Or find an organization that works with seasoned, now retired professionals. It's a great way to get free advice and/or have someone knowledgeable actively assist.

5. Discuss potential issues with your board as a problem solving "group think" at a board meeting.

Bibliography for Chapter 5

Bell, Jeanne and Jan Masaoka. "A Nonprofit Dashboard and Signal Light for Boards." Blue Avocado. July 1, 2009. Accessed March 2017.

The Bridgespan Group. "Refreshing Your Nonprofit Board Dashboard." January 17, 2012.

The Foundation Center. "Tools and Resources for Assessing Social Impact (TRASI)." Philanthropy News Digest. September 28, 2010.

Pope, Elizabeth. "A Few Good CRM Tools." TechSoup. June 24, 2013. Accessed June 2017.

Chapter 6

Write the Vision and Make It Plain: The Importance of a Strategic Plan

Write the vision and make it plain on tablets,
That he may run who reads it.
—Habakkuk 2:2 (NKJV)

THE RIGHT PATH FOR YOUR ORGANIZATION

Nonprofit organizations need strategic plans to guide them through changing times and circumstances. Faith-based nonprofits in the United States are witnessing vast societal changes, and like other organizations, strategies developed by faith-based nonprofits should grow out of their missions. It is possible and indeed necessary to develop a plan that is both rooted in the spiritual beliefs of the community and designed for growth and sustainability. A specific and flexible strategic plan needs the buy-in of both staff and board, and to get that consensus, these stakeholders must be included in the plan's formation.

> "Planning is bringing the future into the present so that you can do something about it now."
>
> —ALAN LAKEIN

Nobody has a crystal ball. In fact, the Bible warns us against soothsayers and false prognosticators. But you can and should have the next best thing: a strategic plan. This is the compass that will help you navigate uncertain terrain, informing decisions large and small, so that you're not going in circles. The strategic plan is a specific and flexible document (I'll explore the meaning of these descriptions later) that brings your mission to life for the period of time under consideration—but not more than three years. The civic, political, and technological landscape is changing at a rapid pace. A strategic planning consultant can be very useful in helping you see the big picture, especially since you are busy facing day-to-day challenges. You need someone who has the experience and understands the objective and the micro issues that you face every day.

Executive leaders make dozens of choices every week. These decisions range from whom to hire (or fire), whether to travel for a conference, and how much to spend on office space. At the same time, small, medium, and large organizations alike exist in an environment of nearly constant change. Economic news, technological possibilities, political vicissitudes, and other factors all mean that yesterday's sound decision can be tomorrow's obsolete strategy.

Think of Christ's Sermon on the Mount as the mission, and this Sunday's sermon at your church as the strategic plan.

> "If anyone will piously and soberly consider the sermon which our Lord Jesus Christ spoke on the mount, as we read it in the Gospel according to Matthew, I think that he will find in it, so far as regards the highest morals, a perfect standard of the Christian life . . ."
>
> ST. AUGUSTINE, On the Sermon on the Mount,
> Book I, chapter 1

The compassion and spirituality in the Sermon on the Mount serve as the foundation or "perfect standard" of how we ought to live our lives. The sermon the minister gives on Sunday, by comparison, takes the teachings of Jesus and applies them to a timely issue for how to live *right now*. He may explore a news event, explain a holiday, or ponder an occurrence in the community that yielded a new realization. If you collect a series of sermons, you may see variations in theme and tone from Sunday to Sunday, but there is a consistency rooted in the mission as set forth by Jesus.

Similarly, the strategic plan takes a variety of factors into account and spells out a way forward for the organization. The Operational Plan that emanates from the Strategic Plan is similar to the sermon. It is the day to day, week to week tracking of the overall plan.

BEGIN WITH WHAT YOU BELIEVE AND WHY YOU EXIST

What do you believe? It's a question I have asked hundreds of organizations. My first foray into this type of inquiry was quite surprising. Many organizations took more than several hours to answer the question because they mistakenly thought the answer was their mission statement. Not so. A good example of capturing what you believe as an organization sounds something like this: "We believe that everyone has the God-given right to drink safe drinking water" or "We believe that Christ's teachings to feed the hungry and clothe the naked must be made real."

What you believe is the driving force of the mission, vision, values, fundraising, and organizational infrastructure. A faith-based organization is a community of people who share a set of beliefs. They don't agree on everything, of course, and they may not all belong to the same church, but keeping that commonly held belief front and center makes it easier to agree on priorities. And priorities are what drive budgetary and strategic considerations.

"Why" is one of the most powerful words in the English language. It's an express lane to the heart of the matter. We want to advertise our services in the newspaper. Why? We want to hold an extravagant gala. Why? We want to add computer classes on the weekends. Why? "Why" isn't meant to kill good ideas, but it helps you to break expensive habits and liberates you from tired excuses while keeping you focused on the mission.

> "Faith is woven into what we do. What difference are we making in the world? Why are we doing this? We're not after success for the sake of success. Program success is how we articulate our faith."
>
> —David Staal, Former President and CEO, Kids Hope USA

Be Specific and Flexible

Now that you have identified what you believe and why you exist as an organization, you must take the time and be comprehensive in your approach to forming a strategic plan. If you do not take the time, this will be an exercise in strategy for the sake of strategy, not a useful tool. Total organizational engagement is harder than it may seem.

I recommend strategic planning retreats as a means to execute a successful process. A good strategic plan should have the following essentials:

Mission

Vision

SWOT (Strengths, Weaknesses, Opportunities, and Threats)

Strategic Priorities

Organization Comparisons

Time lines

Benchmarks

Milestones

Accountability

Evaluation

One useful means of condensing a lot of information into a short space is a SWOT (Strengths, Weaknesses, Opportunities, and Threats) analysis. This exercise begins with brainstorming the strengths, weaknesses, opportunities, and threats for your organization. The first two are internal factors. The second two are external factors. At first, every suggestion should be included, but as the discussion continues, you should be able to narrow it down to three or four items under each heading.

Strengths (Internally Focused)

Characteristics that give your organization an advantage over others:

- What is your value proposition?

- How does it differentiate you from other organizations providing similar services?

- What do others perceive as your strengths?

Weaknesses (Internally Focused)

Characteristics that place the organization at a disadvantage relative to others:

- What do other organizations that provide similar services do better than you?

- What do others perceive as your weaknesses?

Opportunities (Externally Focused)

Characteristics that your organization can capitalize on or use to its advantage:

- What potential prospects could your organization utilize to its advantage?

- What are some trends or conditions that may positively impact you?

Threats (Externally Focused)

Characteristics beyond your control that could be a disadvantage to your organization:

- What are some of the potential dangers your SWOT analysis can uncover?

- What are some external conditions that can negatively impact you?

A thorough brainstorming of all four areas of the SWOT analysis sets the stage to identify strategic priorities.

The strategic priorities set the tone for implementation of your plan. Depending on the size of the organization, five to ten priorities should be agreed upon by the board and staff. Here are a few examples:

1. Clarify mission
2. Define, expand, and fortify advocacy
3. Develop viable, mission-driven technical assistance programs
4. Build appropriate partnership and collaborative opportunities
5. Diversify fundraising

6. Strengthen governance

7. Fortify organizational infrastructure

8. Engage public through PR and marketing

Your strategic priorities should:

- Leverage your strengths

- Eliminate or minimize the effects of your weaknesses

- Take full advantage of your opportunities

- Position your organization so that the threats facing you can be addressed effectively

After consensus has been reached by the group regarding mission, vision, values, the SWOT analysis, and strategic priorities, the rest of the plan becomes very micro.

Specific objectives are essential for a strategic plan. Vague objectives like "increase our profile" or "help more children" are hard to measure and will only lead to disagreement over whether they have been achieved or not. In contrast, setting a goal of increasing your email list from 800 to 1,500, or the number of third graders in your after-school program from 12 to 20, or requiring a specific board fee of $5,000 leaves no room for debate. It either happened or it didn't. As the saying goes, "What gets measured, gets done." The more specific you can get, the more measurable the objective.

Flexibility is equally important. As previously acknowledged, nobody has a crystal ball. Circumstances beyond your control are bound to arise. One measure of your leadership skills is how well you adapt to change. What if the stock market takes a dive? What if three of your board members quit in one week? What if you or a key staff member becomes ill or disabled? A flexible, strategic plan allows for reconsideration and recalibration in light of new realities. David Staal, president of Kids Hope USA, goes so far as to eschew strategic plans in favor of a "strategic direction," which he believes enables the greatest flexibility.

Some other considerations regarding the strategic plan of your faith-based organization:

- Everybody on staff, from the custodian to the CEO, should know the strategic plan, and its objectives should be discussed at staff meetings every month. Rather than reviewing the entire plan, set aside fifteen to twenty minutes at the meeting for one aspect of the plan, such as clients served, students enrolled, or dollars raised.

- The dashboards should display progress on the objectives set forth in the strategic plan.

- The strategic plan should be revisited annually by the board (see chapter 4) to ensure that the directors still buy into the plan, in light of financial and other realities.

- Make sure that financial forecasts are created in tandem with your strategic planning consultant and CFO. Have a clear understanding of the monetary and nonmonetary resources needed to reach all goals and objectives. Take a stark look at actuals versus projected spending is the linchpin to fundraising plans, board decisions, and organizational growth.

BUILDING STRATEGIC CONSENSUS

Your strategic plan is only useful insofar as all the stakeholders buy into it. Staff may approve of your mission, but if they don't believe in the strategic plan, they won't put their all into it. A board member may like you personally, but if she isn't sold on how you're going to get from point A to point B, she probably won't go out of her way to mention your capital campaign at the country club. A large faith-based organization in Florida that had a track record of good fundraising found itself sputtering with declined giving, undefined programs, and board and paid staff floundering regarding their future direction. I facilitated the strategic planning process with all of its staff and prepared a strategic plan document. The client in turn shared that plan with a donor in California they had been cultivating for several years. The donor was so impressed that he wrote a check for $80,000 on the spot! The generous giver told the executive director of the organization, "I have been waiting to see a plan like this." This encouraged the organization to pursue and secure donations all over the country, which resuscitated its fundraising, reinvigorated the staff and the *mission,* and many lives were changed as a result.

The hardest way to achieve internal consensus, however, is to employ your powers of persuasion. Going from person to person and trying to convince them of the genius of your strategy is only going to wear you out. So, what's the alternative? Simply put, your job as a leader is to invite your stakeholders to the table. Bring them into the process early and often so they feel ownership of the plan. Solicit their feedback and truly listen when they respond. Consider delegating pieces of the strategy to experts within and beyond your organization (consultants with strategic planning expertise to provide guidance would be excellent to include at this juncture), and then fit them together like a puzzle. No matter how brilliant you are, the collective wisdom you can assemble will have a better chance of success.

"A successful strategic planning process will examine and make informed projections about environmental realities to help an organization anticipate and respond to change by clarifying its mission and goals; targeting spending; and reshaping its programs, fundraising and other aspects of operations."

—RICHARD A. MITTENTHAL, TCC Group

And speaking of delegation, if you are too busy to assemble the strategic plan yourself—or if your skill set is strong in other ways—you may want to consider engaging a strategic consultant for some or all of this process. This is one of the most important decisions you can make as a leader. I highly recommend an outside facilitator to guide the consensus-building sessions. Retreats organized for this purpose are highly effective. For more about consultants, see chapter 13.

Questions for Discussion

1. What is the difference between mission and strategy?

2. Why is it important for mission to come first?

3. If you asked three different staff or board members to describe the strategic plan, would you get three different answers? What's a way to achieve greater harmony and understanding of the organization's direction?

4. Who "owns" the strategy in your organization? How do you measure progress toward goals?

5. To what extent is the budget a reflection of your strategic plan? What is the standard by which priorities are measured?

6. What do you think a SWOT analysis would reveal about your board, staff, and leadership?

Steps You Can Take Right Now

1. Create a strategic plan for your own professional life. List your objectives for this year and identify the steps you will take to achieve them. Consider how your faith informs and shapes your plan.

2. Find a partner and have him or her ask you "Why?" every time you finish a sentence regarding your

organization's strategic plan. Record your answers and see if a pattern emerges.

3. Ask a colleague at another organization to share their strategic plan. Or exchange plans with your colleague and compare how they set forth objectives.

4. Collect a few recommendations from colleagues regarding strategic planning consultants. Contact the consultants and ask them about their process and format for the final plan. An unreadable, dense plan doesn't provide the kind of road map you need.

Bibliography for Chapter 6

Lanzerotti, Laura, Jacquelyn Hadley, and Adam Nathan. "Living Into Your Strategic Plan: Tools and Templates Index." The Bridgespan Group. December 8, 2011.

Leonard, Kimberlee. "SWOT Analysis of a Nonprofit Organization." *Houston Chronicle*. Updated June 29, 2018.

Mittenthal, Richard A. "Ten Keys to Successful Strategic Planning for Nonprofit and Foundation Leaders." TCC Group. 2002.

Chapter Seven

He Will Make Room for Your Gifts: Your Annual Giving Program

A man's gift makes room for him, and brings him before great men.
—Proverbs 18:16 (NKJV)

Annual giving is the life blood of every nonprofit organization—it's where major gifts emanate. If you don't have an annual giving program it's probably because you don't know where to start. Maybe your excuse is that your donor base is too small. But God's word says He will make room for your gifts. Some may argue the intent of that scripture, but I want to encourage you to start and you will see the increase.

Your annual giving plan should include unrestricted revenue from special events, unrestricted and restricted revenue from appeals, planned giving, major gifts, and board giving with forecasts for future annual giving years. If you are launching annual giving for the first time, modest gains are to be celebrated. Many organizations mistakenly believe that if they send out a few appeals a year and participate in Giving Tuesday, they have an annual giving program. News flash: This is not a plan. This is a rote way of fundraising that doesn't have a strategy, and strategy is everything! The aim of an annual giving program is to get donors in the habit of giving to you so set your sights on regular communication and strategic fundraising throughout the year.

I have an axiom that I say often: Fundraising Is Not Hunting . . . It's Gardening.

Okay, so let's assume you have very few individual donors in your database. Here's what you should do:

ACQUIRE A LIST

According to Blackbaud, you can rent lists to create a universe of donors. Reputable mail houses such as Hill Donnelly, Reach Marketing, and others could be likely brokers. For consumer email lists, prices run about $100 to $150 CPM (that's "cost per mille," which is fancy-talk for "cost per thousand"). So that's 10 to 15 cents apiece for a one-time rental of the email address. If you want to mail your appeals, the cost of a mailing list depends on the type of list you purchase. An occupant list starts at $12.00 per thousand records. A consumer list starts at $33.66 per thousand records. A business list starts at $45.00 per thousand records. Create a budget. Choose someone who has experience in your market, but also choose someone you like and you work well with. Remember, you will be spending a lot of time with your broker.

DETERMINE WHAT WORKS

You need a circulation plan that has key elements including a budget. Also determine which lists have proven donors who have given to an organization through the mail. There should be a tie-in to your cause. Religious trade magazines, education magazines, and AARP could be considered likely donors to faith-based organizations that support "assisted living" as part of their mission. Make sure that the person who manages your Annual Giving Program is experienced or is going to professional development classes focused on Annual Giving with an emphasis on building your donor base.

DETERMINE HOW MANY TIMES TO ASK FOR DONATIONS DURING AN ANNUAL GIVING PROGRAM

Plan your annual giving program outlining the number of appeals. Seasonality can play an important role in making this decision. For faith-based organizations, religious holidays such as Easter, Ramadan, Yom Kippur, Christmas, and Hanukkah are good seasons. The year-end appeal is essential, and don't forget National Philanthropy Day in November. If you are an organization that provides mentoring, National Mentoring Month is in January, and if your constituency is mainly African American, African American History Month is in February. If you are a shelter for domestic violence and other women's issues, Women's History Month is March. You get my drift. Use these celebratory occasions as fundraising strategies.

ANNUAL GIVING AND FUNDRAISING MANAGEMENT SYSTEMS

How are you keeping up with visits to donors from staff, board members, or volunteers? Do you know if someone contacted a donor last week? Last month? Think about the signal that is sent to donors if two people (I have also seen more than two) from the same organization schedule visits without knowing the last touch point for that donor? The donor expects you to know. It's a demonstration of good management and communication.

The popular software program DonorPerfect is a management system with many tools to help nonprofits to increase their database for fund raising. On average, recurring donors give more money for more consecutive years than single-gift donors.

1. Many young and old donors are more willing and able to show their support by donating smaller amounts every month rather than large one-time gifts.

2. DonorPerfect's Monthly Giving Starter Kit will provide you with a proven fundraising strategy and a robust recurring giving tool that seamlessly syncs donation information with your records in DonorPerfect.

There are plenty of resources to help you make room for the gifts that will come to you when you start an annual giving program.

The following is an example of a three-year plan The Gasby Group team put together for a client: Feel free to use it. It's good.

Three Year Annual Giving Campaign Plan Outline

YEAR ONE: INFRASTRUCTURE

Year one of the plan will focus on developing the necessary infrastructure to provide a good foundation for donor development. This will include working on data hygiene and building donor files, developing a case statement, structuring an annual campaign, implementing portfolio management, and educating the entire organization on fund development to help create a culture of philanthropy.

In addition to building infrastructure, training should be updated to ensure staff and volunteers better understand the connection to fund development efforts.

- **Data hygiene and know thy donor.** I laughingly say that Data Hygiene is not "hosing down your donors to get them clean," but the term is used to describe the cleaning and the upgrading of your donor base to ensure that it is accurate and up-to-date.

   Create data hygiene process and policy:

   How will information be entered and by whom?

   Who has access and at what level?

   Thank-a-thon protocol:

   Establish call night(s) staffed by board members.

   Focus on thanking.

   Ask key questions to build donor base and help you understand why they're giving.

- **Case statement.**

  Adopt a written case statement which is the foundational document for your organization. It includes all the vital information regarding your programs, financials, management, mission and vision. Use the case statement to write proposals, develop messages for social media and your appeals. Your Annual Giving or Campaign Case for Support will be easier to develop when the Case Statement is in place. The Case Statement is also used to develop key talking points throughout the organization.

- **Structure annual campaign.**

  Determine number of written appeals each year.

  Determine the number of newsletters.

  Determine electronic communication schedule.

  Lapsed donor strategy (How to recapture donors who haven't given in the past 2–3 years).

  Donor segmentation strategy (especially major gifts) One size does not fit all. Create different strategies for your various donor segments by age, geography and giving history.

- **Implement portfolio management for donors who meet the Major Gift category.**

  Perform donor analysis and research to build knowledge.

  Make a communication plan for each donor (touchpoints).

  Focus on relationship development and a shared story.

- **Education.**

  Create a culture of philanthropy organization wide. Everyone, from the person who empties the trash, to the chair of the board should know and understand the importance of fundraising to your organization.

Engage in Leadership coaching.

YEAR TWO: REGULAR GIVING

Year two will focus on building regular giving by promoting a circle of friends giving circle, a giving society, and ministry or donor briefings. The giving circle should focus on cultivating monthly giving among smaller donors by providing a way for them to feel a deeper connection with your organization. Studies have shown that donors providing small, regular gifts are ideal candidates for legacy gifts. Focusing on building a consistent group of regular givers creates a good pool of planned giving prospects as well as providing a consistent stream of funds for budgeting purposes. It is also a way to manage annual campaign costs, since circle members will be excluded from regular appeal letters and have the option of receiving an annual tax statement as opposed to regular thank-you note.

Giving circle members should receive segmented communication that may include a once a year thank-you call, a handwritten note from a board member at least annually, special electronic CEO updates exclusively for circle members, and a special year-end appeal. Strategies should be formulated to continue adding new members to the giving circle and increasing annual donations of members.

The giving society, on the other hand, should focus on larger donors giving at the major gift level annually. This group of segmented donors will receive more personal attention that may include: an annual event, handwritten notes, special ministry updates, and regular calls and/or visits from a portfolio manager.

- *Giving Circle of Friends.*

    Develop a giving circle of donors that pledge monthly support with annual giving less than $500 (this number will increase based on the size of your organization).

Establish segmented communication plan for members as a whole.

Plan Annual recognition.

- *Giving Society.*

  Establish larger donor giving society for donors with annual gifts at the major gift level and above.

  Set up segmented communication for members.

  Plan annual recognition event(s).

- *Ministry briefings.*

  Create a briefing kit that can be used by any friend of the ministry to host an at-home event to share your organization's story—the tool kit can be made accessible online for ease of use and affordability.

  Plan multiple events (for national organizations, make sure they can be replicated nationally).

  Ask current donors and friends to host events.

  Focus events on telling the story of your organization and cultivating relationships with current donors and prospective donors.

YEAR THREE: EXPANDING THE NETWORK

Year three will continue building on the work already established to expand the network. This will include focused acquisition strategies to build the donor base, as well as expanded ministry briefings to further develop existing donor relationships and cultivate new prospect relationships.

- *Pay for lists for year-end mailing.*

  Use outside vendor for targeted acquisition mailings.

  Buy clean, qualified lists.

- *Expanded ministry briefings.*

    Provide training in all markets (if national).

    Implement regular ministry briefings in all communities.

    Promote plan to engage others in hosting ministry briefings around the country.

- *Planned giving strategy.*

    Include legacy language in all communications.

    Implement annual planned giving appeal to segmented donors, particularly focused on giving circle members.

Take what you need from this plan and apply it. You will definitely see results.

Questions for Discussion

1. What is the audience we want to reach?
2. Are there multiple audiences with different interests?
3. How many donors can we manage at one time?
4. What kind of software will we use to track our donors?
5. Do we need to bring on a consultant to help us in the initial stages?
6. Who will manage the Annual Giving Program?
7. Are we prepared to lose money the first year or more in order to raise money in the future?

Steps You Can Take Right Now

1. Ask your Development Committee of the board to make recommendations regarding an Annual Giving Program.

2. Ask your Finance Committee to make initial recommendations regarding costs based on your budget (We can't do it is NOT an answer).

3. Study annual giving of other organizations.

Bibliography for Chapter 7

Newell, Susan. "All About Lists: What Every Fundraiser Should Know," Target Analytics, a Blackbaud Company. Accessed PDF file September 2018.

Brown, M. Gasby. "A Sample Faith-Based Annual Giving Program." The Gasby Group, Inc.

Chapter Eight

The Fundraising Business of Your Community Development Corporation: To Rely or Not to Rely on Your Church for Funding

¹¹ *And he gave the apostles, the prophets, the evangelists, the shepherds and teachers,*

¹² *to equip the saints for the work of ministry, for building up the body of Christ,*

¹³ *until we all attain the unity of the faith and of the knowledge of the Son of God.*

—Ephesians 4:11, 12 and 13

If your faith-based organization is an outgrowth of your church, can and should you expect that they will provide funding? If the answer is yes, how do you go about seeking funding from your church? Before seeking funding, you should be aware of the church's procedure and guidelines for applying for and receiving funds.

First, consider whether your faith-based group would qualify for funding from the church from which it was an outgrowth. Does your church/synagogue/mosque only fund programs affiliated with the denomination or religion, or do they have a history of funding other community groups? Does your church already have funding priorities or internal restrictions regarding the types of groups it funds? For example, if your church is focusing on groups working in the area of health care for the current year and you are seeking funding for your faith-based organization, which feeds needy community members,

your organization may not fit within your church's funding priorities. Does your faith-based organization pay salaries for congregation members? Your church may have an anti-nepotism policy about
funding groups that employ members of the congregation.

If you think you may qualify for church funding, you should
familiarize yourself with your church's process for applying for funds
to ensure that you meet all deadlines and provide church decision
makers with sufficient information. Will you be subject to the same
funding application process as other faith-based groups desiring
church support, or might your application for funding be subject to
a different process because you are an outgrowth of the church? If
you do need to follow the same process as other groups you should
know the group that is your church's deciding body for the potential funding of faith-based groups and when this group makes its
decisions regarding funding. Does this deciding body have regular
meetings, and if so, are they open to other members of the church
community to attend? If so, it may be wise for you and possibly others who work with your faith-based organization to attend a meeting
to get a flavor for the deciding group and its priorities.

If appropriate, you may want to ask to give a presentation about
the work of your faith-based group to the deciding body to make
sure they are aware of your wonderful past work as well as upcom-
ing programs. You should be realistic about the support your church
can provide, as there are many yearly church needs (e.g. building
and maintenance, pastor salaries) and there may be a number of
other individuals in your church connected with nonprofit groups
desiring funding.

If your faith-based organization is in a situation where there is
great need for a particular project or you are in danger of shutting
down for lack of funds, you may want to appeal to the church for
funding outside of the regular funding cycle. Does your church have
an emergency fund? Before asking for emergency funds or funds

outside of the normal cycle make sure that it really is an emergency, as applying for funding in this fashion may cause your group to be viewed in a different and possibly more negative light. Additionally, applying for emergency funding is something that you do not want to do many times, if at all.

There are a number of reasons to apply to your church for funding. It is natural that your church would wish to continue their relationship with an organization that was an outgrowth of it through financial support, as the church is likely very proud of the work your organization does. Your organization may fit within your church's goals for community assistance and/or funding priorities, which would create a strong win-win situation for the church and your faith-based organization. If your church is financially solvent and regularly gives donations to faith-based groups, it could be a reliable source of funding that you can count on year after year.

Although your church can be a natural source of funding, make sure that you are not overly reliant on it. It is so important to diversify your organization's fundraising sources. Financial troubles the church might encounter or a change in church funding priorities or leadership could cause a decrease or complete cessation of funding to your organization. There could also be internal church politics that might make church funding during a particular year or funding at all unwise. Can you get by without church funding? If so, your church likely receives many funding requests, and there may be other groups that have a greater need for funds than yours at a particular time. In that case, if there are not enough funds for everyone, it may be wise to step aside and let these other groups receive the funds. It's also worth considering that certain individuals associated with your church or clients of your organization might be put off by too close of an alliance with a particular church or denomination.

You should also be aware that many churches do not spend a large portion of their budget and staff time on social service projects such as those undertaken by your faith-based organization. Individual congregational involvement in social services greatly varies amongst congregations. In 2001 only 6 percent of congregations had a staff person devoting at least a quarter of his or her time to social service projects. The median amount spent by congregations directly in support of social support programs was about $1,200, which was about three percent of the congregation's budget. An average of ten people per church do volunteer work connected with a congregation's social services.

It is important to understand some of the mission priorities of individual denominations. Your organization may fit within the priorities of a particular mission. Even if you are outside of that mission's priorities, it may be wise to have a sense of the types of mission work some denominations are already funding before you start to seek funds from your denomination.

A deep commitment to mission is part of the identity of the American Baptist Church, and they organized their several mission programs very effectively. A program of the organization called "American Baptist Mission Support" is the grand total of all money given by the American Baptist church to mission and totals over $40 million a year. The largest portion of the mission budget is for "United Mission," which is typically part of an individual church's budget and may be part of a tithe or offering. Sixty-five percent of United Mission supports regional ministries, eight percent supports general ministries, and seven percent supports international ministries. Congregations may give both undesignated gifts to United Mission as well as gifts designated for a particular budgeted regional, national, or general American Baptist mission or ministry.

"United Mission Love Gifts" are contributions from American Baptist women in support of a particular American Baptist ministry. In 2003 the American Baptist general board approved a new common budget covenant agreement in which regions could continue mission support by continuing to use the United Mission foundational model of giving or else formulate their own giving strategy with a flexible stewardship plan. The majority of regions in the country still use the United Mission system for mission funding. However, some churches have customized the model through which they raise and use funds for mission and now use their own funding models alongside funding for United Mission.

The "America for Christ Offering" is the American Baptist response to the needs of America, both within and beyond the local congregation. Gifts are channeled through national and regional ministries to fund mission within the United States, education, and local community ministries.

The Episcopal Church has also developed a denominational model for mission. Through a multiyear process of prayer, reflection, and thoughtful consideration, the Episcopal Church developed five funding areas as a means of advancing the church's worldwide mission priorities: the fund for congregational development, the fund for global ministries, the fund for communications, the fund for leadership, and the fund for spiritual enrichment. In addition to these funds, the church has a campaign for the Archives and Mission Research Center. The Episcopal Church also established the St. Ives Fund to support the church's unity and preserve its heritage. Additionally, Episcopal Relief and Development is the church's response to human suffering. It is an independent nonprofit affiliated with the Episcopal Church.

The United Methodist Church is the second largest Protestant denomination in the United States. The United Methodist Church created the General Board of Global Ministries (GBGM) as the church's global mission agency. GBGM is organized in four units: Mission and Evangelism, Development and Communication, the United Methodist Committee on Relief (UMCOR), and the Women's Division. A major area of focus for the denomination is the

Global Health Initiative, which aims to combat diseases of poverty including malaria, HIV/AIDS, and tuberculosis. It also provides health education, advocacy, and infrastructure.

The Methodist Church has a program called "The Advance," which allows congregants to give to any United Methodist ministry of their choice. Donations can be made online, through the church, or via phone or mail. Of each gift received, 100 percent will reach the intended ministry. Individual United Methodist churches may have a mission council, treasury, or other body that annually meets to decide which local, national, and global ministries the church wishes to support. The money this group will give to faith-based and secular nonprofits comes from congregants who have donated as well as from general church budgetary funds that have been designated for mission. This body may also handle one-time appeals from faith-based groups for specific needs.

The Office of Adventist Mission was formed in 2005 at the Seventh-day Adventist world convention in St. Louis. Adventist Mission is currently active in 204 countries. The mission is dedicated to meeting the physical and emotional needs of individuals throughout the world and has programs such as teaching life skills, providing health care at hospitals and clinics, conducting development projects, and supplying resources and organizational support.

The Adventist Development and Relief Agency is an international development and relief agency established by the Seventh-Day Adventist Church. In 2008 alone it assisted more than 20 million people with $120 million in aid. Other Seventh-day Adventist missions include the Global Mission, which takes the message of Jesus's love to people around the world; the Department of Public Affairs and Religious Liberty; the Education division, which works with Adventist schools, colleges, and universities; as well as Health, Volunteer Services, and Adventist Media.

Questions for Discussion

1. From what sources can my fundraising be most effective?
2. How much congregational and denominational funding can we expect?
3. Can the board set the tone for diversifying our fundraising?

Steps You Can Take Right Now

1. Call a meeting with your Development Committee to discuss funding sources and sustainability.
2. Consider a Development Audit conducted by an outside consultant.
3. Reach out to other leaders of faith-based nonprofits who have successfully navigated the issue.

Bibliography for Chapter 8

American Baptist Churches USA. "Funding the Mission." Accessed February 7, 2011. http://www.abc-usa.org/what_we_believe/mission/mission-giving/funding-the-mission/

Chaves, Mark. "Six Myths About Faith-Based Initiatives." Religion-Online. The Christian Century Foundation. 2001. https://www.religion-online.org/article/six-myths-about-faith-based-initiatives/

The Episcopal Church. "Mission Funding." The Episcopal Church Welcomes You. 2008. http://www.episcopalchurch.org/mission_funding.htm.

Seventh-Day Adventist Church. "ADRA: Adventist Development and Relief Agency." General Conference of Seventh-day Adventists. Accessed February 7, 2011. http://www.adventist.org/mission-and-service/adra.html.

The United Methodist Church. Global Ministries: The United Methodist Church. Accessed February 7, 2011. https://www.umcmission.org/

Weekly, Rev. David. "Open Hearts, Open minds, Open doors: The People of The United Methodist Church." Reconciling Ministries Network. May 15, 2009. https://rmnetwork.org/open-hearts-open-minds-open-doors-the-people-of-the-united-methodist-church/

Chapter 9

The Fundraising Business of Your Faith-Based School: The Bake Sale Will Never Be Enough

And my God will supply your every need according to his glorious riches in Christ Jesus.
—Philippians 4:19
New English Translation (NET)

If you are running a faith based nonprofit school, this chapter is for you. Bake sales, bazaars, and art festivals (also featuring baked goods), and candy and cookie-sale campaigns are too often the primary fundraising strategies for faith-based schools. These methods will never be enough. It's time to expand your fundraising thinking. The costs of running a faith-based school can be very steep, and there are many potential sources to fund their operations, educational programs and scholarship needs Some sources of funding are very traditional, while others may be more creative or unexpected.

SUCCESS STORIES

It is interesting to look at some successful faith-based schools to learn how they receive their funding. One is the Wesleyan School that was established in 1963 as part of Sandy Springs United Methodist Church in Georgia. The school was initially a preschool dedicated to providing a nurturing, educational experience guided by Christian principles. Over the next twenty-four years the school was housed at the church and led by pastors and lay directors. During this time the school grew to include elementary school students. In the 1970s the school emerged as an elementary school of excellence grounded in

Christian principles. In 1994 the school added a high school curriculum, and in 1996 the school opened its new building on a 53-acre site in Peachtree Corners for the 556 students on its campus.

Much of the funding of Wesleyan comes from the families of students who attend the school. The school has an online form for donations. Instead of raising the cost of tuition to cover all of the expenses, the school decided to have an ongoing annual fund to keep tuition costs affordable for more families. Tuition at Wesleyan only covers 90 percent of the true cost of a Wesleyan education, and gifts to the annual fund from parents, friends, faculty, staff, and alumni are used to supplement tuition costs. In December 2003 the school had a "Raise the Goal" campaign that raised $45 million. They also started their final building campaign and first major endowment campaign, called "Complete the Campus." This campaign had a goal of $42 million including $10.4 million for the endowment, $7 million of which would fund financial aid. The normal pledge period for a building or endowment campaign is four years. Fundraising at Wesleyan includes a high rate of parent participation—there was an average of 95 percent parent participation in capital campaigns from 2001 to 2010.

Atlanta Jewish Academy was incorporated on July 1, 2014, as a result of the merger of Greenfield Hebrew Academy (GHA) and Yeshiva Atlanta (YA)—the oldest Jewish day schools in Atlanta. Founded in 1953, GHA had a history of distinction and achievement. GHA was the first Jewish day school in the country to be accredited by the Southern Association of Colleges and Schools, and it was twice honored as a National School of Excellence by the Council for American Private Education. GHA also won the highly respected Jerusalem Prize for exemplary achievement in Zionist and Torah Education; this is administered by the World Zionist Organization. GHA's founders fervently believed the timeless values of the Jewish community transcended the differences among denominations. They envisioned and built a school where all could be respected, learn from each other and work toward their community's greater good.

Yeshiva Atlanta was founded in 1971, it became Atlanta's oldest coeducational Jewish high school with a remarkable record of academic achievement. YA understood that adolescent growth involves four areas: intellectual, social-emotional, physical, and religious-spiritual. To nurture the well-rounded student, the school promoted participation in sports, fine arts, and service learning in addition to academic excellence. YA's nurturing environment offered many opportunities for students to develop their own identities, both in the secular world and the Jewish community. The merger of GHA and YA combined the best of both schools.

Atlanta Jewish Academy offers classes to students from early childhood through 12th grade and helps them on their Jewish education journey. AJA has a new gym is under construction. The Minsk Gymnasium will be complete in December 2018, and their Jaguars will enjoy their new home in this state-of-the-art gym. New Jewish-based, social and team-building programs are being created through the Vivian Zisholtz Sportsmanship Center. Now that Phase 1—their new Upper School Building—is complete and with no permanent debt, it will be time for Phase 2.

As of September 2018, AJA had achieved more than 80 percent of its fundraising goal and looked to close out the capital campaign in December 2018. AJA incorporated naming opportunities:

OPPORTUNITY	AMOUNT
Gym Lobby	$250,000
Wrestling Room	$150,000
Entrance Gate	$100,000
Weight Room	$100,000
Scoreboards	$50,000

(continued)

OPPORTUNITY	AMOUNT
Women's Locker Room	$50,000
Men's Locker Room	$50,000
Atheletic Director's Office	$25,000
Gym Bleachers (2)	$25,000 each
Mezuzah (7)	$10,000 each

No bake sales to raise money here. They are engaging in smart fundraising on a number of levels.

Hamzah Academy, a full-time Islamic School located in Alpharetta, Georgia, is currently facing all the challenges of our society, but is responding to high academic expectations despite its lack of finances. In addition to tuition revenue, they explored alternative ways such as approaching a new circle of donors to bring steady income to the school.

They had relied on their local community. However, to maintain their high standard and complete their future projects they needed help from the extended community. They made the case for taking Hamzah to the next level, by nurturing the next generation to become leaders as teachers, engineers, doctors, and other professionals.

By speaking to the best possible return on investment, their case for support was strong. It emphasized the need for donors to help build the foundation for a strong new Muslim generation and expressed their belief that Allah (SWT) will reward them abundantly for their support of this noble cause. Who could argue with that approach? Their 2018 fundraising campaign to raise $60,000 includes expanding their donor base beyond their immediate community. What a savvy way to diversify their fundraising to meet their operational budget and goals.

Cristo Ray is a Catholic high school located in Detroit that has a different funding model. The school emphasizes faith, morals, and service to the community and a college preparatory education. Families of children who attend the school pay tuition on a sliding scale based on their income, and no family pays more than $2,350 a year per student for tuition. Additionally, the school offers up to $2,000 in financial aid per student. Families who belong to any parish in Detroit are eligible for up to $700 additional in financial aid through the Archdiocese of Detroit. Five days a month, students work outside the classroom and receive two-thirds of their tuition as well as the benefit of work experience. Work-study sponsors include a diverse array of groups, including the church, faith-based nonprofits, secular nonprofits, as well as financial, legal, entertainment, health care, insurance, and education groups. The remaining tuition is paid by family members and fundraising.

About thirty miles away from Detroit, Huron Valley Catholic School in Ypsilanti, Michigan, is aware that the tuition-based model of fundraising does not work for all private Christian schools. There are 185 students enrolled in kindergarten through eighth grade at Huron Valley, but the school knows that to be economically viable it must increase its enrollment to above 210 students. The school's principal, Timothy Kotyuk, noted that not having a lot of turnover is important for their fundraising efforts. Elementary school tuition is lower than high school tuition, and tuition only makes up 60 percent of the school's income. Increasing the number of students isn't the only step the school is taking to raise additional funds. The school stepped up its major fundraiser, a dinner auction, and a new development committee was formed to look for support from sources outside the school's 110 families. Fundraising amounted to 15 percent, donations earmarked for scholarships were 11 percent, and at-large donations were 10 percent.

GOVERNMENT FUNDING OPPORTUNITIES

The federal government is a source that some faith-based schools look to for funding. Most government grants to schools come from the Department of Education. There are some grants for private schools available through funds from the American Recovery and Reinvestment Act of 2009, or "stimulus." Of course the political climate will often affect how such funds are dispersed.

Another source of federal funding for faith-based schools is the Center for Faith-based and Neighborhood Partnerships, which is part of the United States Department of Health and Human Services and serves as the Department's liaison to grassroots organizations. According to their website, while there is no specific "faith-based" funding, the center works to enable community and faith-based organizations to partner with the government through both fiduciary and nonfiduciary relationships to achieve the goals of the Faith-based and Neighborhood Partnership Initiative. The goals of this initiative are to: (1) strengthen the role of community organization in economic recovery and reducing poverty, (2) reduce unintended pregnancies and support maternal and child health, (3) promote responsible fatherhood and healthy families, and (4) foster interfaith dialogue and collaboration with leaders and scholars around the world and at home. The center offers resources, including grant opportunities, for faith-based organizations.

How is the process of applying for a federal grant different than applications for other types of grants? Applying for federal funding can be complex and requires significant energy and effort. Many private funding sources, such as foundations and for-profit corporations, require only brief proposals that are a few pages for very a very specific focus. Federal grants have multiple goals, specific program requirements, and require compliance with government-wide standards. Prior to receiving federal funding, you must have received and maintained your status as a 501(c)(3) nonprofit. This will likely be a requirement for other types of grants as well.

You must also determine whether you meet the specific program requirements. For example, some programs require a number of years working with a certain population or providing a specific service, while others only accept applications from grantees who have never received federal funds. As each Federal agency has its own eligibility requirements, if possible, you may want to attend technical assistance workshops sponsored by the Agency offering the grant or, if you cannot attend, request the workshop material. Make sure that there is a need for your program that can be documented and supported by statistical data.

There are two websites you should be aware of when applying for federal grants. The Catalog of Federal Domestic Assistance (CFDA), www.cfda.gov, is a government-wide list of federal programs, projects, services, and activities that provide assistance or benefits. The website contains both financial and nonfinancial assistance programs administered by the Federal government. On this website, you can search for grants and as well as read more about writing a grant proposal. CFDA includes non-monetary forms of assistance in addition to grants, but and you cannot apply for these on the website.

The federal website solely focused on financial gifts from the federal government is www.grants.gov, which contains a list of all discretionary grants being offered by the federal government and is the source for applying for federal grants. It is a central storehouse for information on over 1,000 grant programs and over $500 billion in annual awards. On the www.grants.gov website you can also sign up for a notification service, which will notify you regarding program announcements, deadlines, and changes in grant programs that you are interested in. If you have any questions about a specific grant, you can contact the official listed in the "request for application or program announcement" section.

In addition to grants, the federal government often sponsors school vouchers, which are grants made to individual families who wish to enroll their child in a private school. This indirectly provides federal funding to faith-based schools.

States, county, and city governments may also offer grants for faith-based schools. A good place to start searching for these grants is on state websites, including the State Education Agency. You can search for local grants by visiting local government websites as well as calling local departments of education or treasury departments.

Questions for Discussion

1. How should we look at our current approach to raising money?
2. If the Golf Tournament, Dinner, Bake Sale or Bazaar is not raising enough money should we eliminate them?
3. How can we best meet our budget and have reserves without raising tuition?
4. Is an endowment campaign feasible for us at this time?
5. How do we build relationships with major donors and Foundation Program Officers?

Steps You Can Take Right Now

1. Analyze your current donor base.
2. Discuss diversifying your fundraising strategy with your board.
3. Develop a Strategic Fundraising Plan.
4. Research Foundation Program Officers who fund faith-based organizations in your area.

Bibliography for Chapter 9

Atlanta Jewish Academy. "About Us." Accessed website September 2018.

Atlanta Jewish Academy. "Capital Campaign." Accessed website September 2018.

Catalog of Federal Domestic Assistance. "CFDA Overview." Accessed website February 9, 2011.

Center for Faith-Based and Neighborhood Partnerships. "About Faith-Based and Neighborhood Partnerships." Department of Health and Human Services. October 26, 2017.

Detroit Cristo Rey High School. "Mission Statement." Accessed website February 9, 2011.

Detroit Cristo Ray High School. "Our Partners: Corporate Work Study Program Partners." Accessed website August 2017.

Detroit Cristo Rey High School. "The School that Works." Accessed August 2017.

Hamzah Academy. "About Us" Accessed website September 2018.

Hamzah Academy. "Giving" Accessed website September 2018.

Morley, Miranda. "Agencies That Give Grants to Churches." Disfluent. Updated September 26, 2017.

Office of Management and Budget. "About Grants.gov." Add access date. http://www.grants.gov/aboutgrants/about_grants_gov.jsp.

Shane, Lorie A. "Private schools cope with weak economy: Tuition model isn't enough; schools look to broaden revenue sources." Mackinac Center for Public Policy. May 26, 2010.

U.S. Department of Health and Human Services. "Acquiring Public Grants." Compassion Capital Fund National Resource Center. Accessed website February 9, 2011.

U.S. Department of Health and Human Services. "Developing a Competitive SAMHSA Grant Application." Substance Abuse and Mental Health Services Administration. Modified February 2018.

U.S. Department of Health and Human Services. "How to Apply for Grants." Accessed February 9, 2011.

Walden University. "Grants for Starting a Private School." The Richard W. Riley College of Education and Leadership. 2010.

Wesleyan School. "Annual Fund FAQs." Accessed website February 9, 2011.

Wesleyan School. "Complete the Campus Campaign." Accessed website February 9, 2011.

Wesleyan School. "Endowment Components. Accessed website February 9, 2011.

Wesleyan School. "Welcome to Wesleyan School." Last modified May 1, 2018.

Chapter Ten

Fundraising Soup for the Soul: Major Gifts, Events, Corporations, Foundations, and Social Media

Commit your works to the Lord, And your thoughts will be established.
—Proverbs 16:3 (NKJV)

LOOKING AT THE RETURN ON YOUR ORGANIZATIONAL INVESTMENT

There are many vehicles to use in fundraising for your organization. All too often, the reliance is on "fundraisers," which are really special events with the hope of raising money. The dinner, gala, or golf tournament are all mostly high effort/low yield fundraising events and contribute marginally to your annual operating budget. There are a small percentage of nonprofit organizations who do this well. Other vehicles, such as major gifts and foundation and corporate giving should be strategically considered and implemented.

According to Jim Greenfield and the Association of Fundraising Professionals, the ROI of various fundraising vehicles looks like this:

RETURN ON INVESTMENT PER FUNDRAISING VEHICLE		
VEHICLE	**CRD**	**ROI**
Direct Mail (General List)	115%	-15%
Special Events	50%	50%
Planned Giving	25%	75%

(continued)

RETURN ON INVESTMENT PER FUNDRAISING VEHICLE		
VEHICLE	CRD	ROI
Direct Mail (Previous Donors)	20%	80%
Foundations/Corporations	20%	80%
Major Gifts	5–10%	90–95%
Average	20%	80%

MAJOR GIFTS FROM INDIVIDUALS

Major gift giving is all about relationships. Successful major gift programs are dependent on the art of fundraising. Yes, the data for each individual based on careful prospect research is important, but the ultimate solicitation is based on the "art" of a slow and intentional relationship.

According to Wikipedia, as a counter to the growing fast-food juggernaut, Carlo Petrini founded Slow Food in Italy in 1986. It was promoted as an alternative to fast food. Its goal was to preserve traditional and regional cuisine. It has since spread worldwide, and to this day it encourages farming based on local ecosystems.

Now society again finds itself grappling with a once socially connective component accelerated to a breakneck pace—this time it is relationships. Relationships have jumped to the warp speed of social media. Millennials seem to live on social media, and many nonprofit organizations are embracing digital fundraising as the answer to capturing the elusive attention of millennials.

Social media has its place in the fundraising mix. For larger and more substantial giving, however, it is time for a new movement. Taking a cue from Slow Food, let's call it "slow relationships." We need to be more intentional about moving from the quick and superficial to more meaningful interactions with potential donors.

What defines slow relationships versus fast relationships? Slow relationships talk in full sentences, for one! Slow relationships take a genuine interest in the other person. We can see the detrimental effects of fast relationships in American political landscapes today. Both sides of the aisle acknowledge we have never seen so much polarization among people in the United States. Slow relationships are needed in every sphere within our society; the country is literally starving for more meaningful connections.

The fundraising industry and the nonprofit sector have a unique opportunity to lead the way for the slow relationships movement. Who else would be better suited? According to the National Center for Charitable Statistics (NCCS), more than 1.5 million nonprofit organizations are registered in the United States. The majority of them need to diversify and expand their major gift funding sources.

This is another unique opportunity as slow relationships promote diversity. All kinds of individuals who haven't been perceived as able or interested in giving in the past often open up their hearts, minds, and wallets when approached through the paradigm of slow relationships. The 2016 U.S. Trust Study of High Net Worth Philanthropy has identified growth in giving from African Americans, Latinos, Hispanics, Asian Americans, and LBGTs. Many of these donors are unfamiliar with the nonprofits who hope to reach them and who might be a very good fit. Social media is not enough—these groups need to be introduced to philanthropic opportunities through slow relationships. We know that relationships are at the heart of major gifts, and these are the gifts that will be needed to fill the anticipated fundraising gaps. The major gift level for donors is what nonprofit organizations desire most as they move from first-time gifts to renewal gifts, to upgrade gifts, to special gifts, and finally major gifts. These new donors, just like any others, need to feel listened to, valued, and that they have a seat at the table.

Just think about the impact nonprofit organizations will have on communication with all types of donors with slow relationships. This increase in communication could aid in bridging cultural gaps and the divisiveness we currently face because of a lack of meaningful exposure to people who are different from us (in terms of color, ethnicity, economic status, and so on).

Yes, LinkedIn and Twitter and other platforms allow for more relationships than ever before, but social media is, by its very nature, broad but shallow. Nonprofits need, more than ever, to go back to the time-tested historic art of fundraising.

When it comes to cultivating donors and building slow, long-lasting relationships, the notion of slow relationships is actually not new but is one of the three parts of the art of successful fundraising. These three parts are the art of listening, the art of understanding, and the art of meaningful, slow relationships.

As fundraising professionals, we do more than just help fund organizations—far more. We are the ones responsible for ensuring that the resources of the donor go to the organization that can help realize their highest aspirations. This is a sacred trust. And this is why slow relationships are so important. This kind of trust cannot be formed over a relationship online.

We need to know the donor's deepest dreams for building a better world. We need to listen without thought for ourselves, we need to understand how and why donors give, and finally we need to weave all of this into a relationship of mutual respect. All this amounts to a need to have deep, long-lasting relationships with donors— slow relationships.

Beyond the "likes" and retweets, there is a type of connection that C. S. Lewis described as one of discovery, a kind of meeting of minds (or dare I say, souls) that exclaims, "What! You too? I thought I was the only one [who felt that way about it]!" Or as Saint Francis of Assisi described it, "to seek to understand and to be understood." That can only be accomplished in a slow relationship.

Nonprofits today need to slow down in order to move ahead and lead the way.

What qualifies as a major gift varies. For one organization it could be $500, for another $50,000. The board can set the bar for the level. For a small faith-based nonprofit that is building a donor base, the major gifts level would be expected to be lower until the number of gifts significantly increase. For a mid-sized organization that can track donors for at least three years, the major gift level would be higher. For the large nonprofit that already has an established donor base and tracking system for the past five years, the major gift level would be higher. Whatever the level is, the time and effort in establishing relationships with major donors and potential ones is very important.

MAJOR GIFT CULTIVATION AND SOLICITATION

Who should spend the time to build a major gifts donor base? No matter what the size of the organization is, the president or executive director and board hold the bulk of the responsibility. With mid-sized and larger organizations, "Major Gift or Leadership Gift Officers" are needed. They have portfolios and goals they must reach every year. These fundraising professionals should be evaluated on the number of major gifts they renewed, the number of new gifts they secured, and the number of potential donors they have identified, qualified, and cultivated. Stewardship is a big piece of their work as well. These MG Officers should be good at what they do, but remember that cultivation takes time.

If your organization is just beginning to build your major gifts program, please avoid having unrealistic expectation of the staff you hired. Make sure that they have the support they need to do their jobs:

- Board members who can make connections

- A prospect researcher who can provide valuable information on the prospective donor

- A software management system that can track touch points with each MG donor
- A philanthropic culture within the organization

After the gift is given, also do your part to recognize these donors as much as you can. If they want to remain anonymous, by all means respect their wishes.

FOUNDATIONS AND CORPORATIONS

The first hurdle to overcome in these categories is to make sure they have an affinity for faith-based organizations. Many don't, and some do. Make sure you have researched their guidelines to ensure a match of their interests and your cause. You also want to make sure their products and values are compatible with yours. All money is not good money when it comes to faith-based organizations. What is your written policy about accepting money? For example: Will you accept gifts from alcohol and tobacco companies?

BEST PRACTICES FOR
GRANT APPLICATIONS FOUNDATIONS

I have discussed the many different sources of funding for faith-based schools around the country. It's now important to turn to some of the principles that faith-based schools and other faith-based groups should keep in mind when they are applying for grants from foundations.

Foundations may be a source of funding for a faith-based school if the school is aimed at serving a minority or disadvantaged population. Some foundations, such as the Lilly Endowment, specifically fund faith-based endeavors. Much of the work of successful grantees begins before grants are even announced. If you are not familiar with grant applications, take some time to read grant announcements.

This will familiarize you with the language used in grants. Begin grant application groundwork before grant announcements are published, and keep a close watch on groups or databases where relevant grants are routinely published. Pay attention to emerging grant programs that match your interests or needs that will likely offer grants later. Be sure to research and monitor relevant grant programs and funding cycles. You may want to keep a notebook or file of potential groups that may later have grants that match your needs.

You should be prepared to start writing a grant application as soon as the time for application starts, as many grants have a short time frame in which to apply. Create a list of contacts that can assist with grant writing, and consider creating a committee to assist with developing grant applications. Identify individuals who can complete the various tasks involved in applying for a grant, such as writing the application, critiquing the application, and identifying questions or gaps. And, if required, you may need someone to write individual letters of support describing how your organization can contribute to the goals of the grantor organization. Although several people may write portions of a grant application, one person should put the entire grant together to ensure that it flows well.

Once a grant is announced, you should first ensure that you really are a strong candidate for the grant before applying. Do not apply for a grant unless it is truly consistent with your mission and your organization has the capacity to complete the application and successfully manage the funds should you be funded. For a successful grant application, you must be able to match your ideas to the funding source and thoroughly understand the goals of the grant program to which you are applying.

Once a grant is announced, establish a timetable for your application and organize the necessary personnel immediately. Do not miss a deadline or your application will be rejected, and use all available resources in writing your grant application. The grantor may have resources available to assist grantees, and, if this is the case, make sure to take advantage of these resources for your application. Make a reasonable funding request from the grantor based on your budget. Your justification for funds must match the amount requested.

Be sure to follow all instructions regarding submitting your application, and do not stray from the application format. Also pay attention to all formatting requirements, including page limits, font size, and the number of copies required for submission.

When writing the grant application, make sure you lay out a master plan that includes a vision of where your project is going and the expected results. The application should cover the basics of your project including who, what, where, when, and why. A good grant application will include your project objective(s), tasks required to accomplish the objectives, target population, resources, time frames, and the methodology by which you evaluate your accomplishments. You may want to include other funding sources and what the funding from those sources actually covers, as often a grant from a reputable source will cause other grantees to look more favorably upon your organization. Be succinct, and do not provide unnecessary detail. Include evidence as to how you can achieve your goals.

Your completed application should be simple, reasonable, business-like, and professional. There should be no misspellings or omitted sections, and you should have followed all directions in the grant announcement documents.

Some family foundations have a specific focus on faith-based missions. Do your research.

The Society for Nonprofits is a national membership association that provides valuable resources including articles, educational programs, grant information, fundraising guides, and job listings. Learn more at www.snpo.org.

Working with the Society for Nonprofits we updated their wonderful comprehensive list of family foundations. It was updated

March 15, 2019. The following list are some of the family foundations who give to faith-based organizations:

AARON AND MARIE BLACKMAN FOUNDATION

The Foundation, established in 1989, focuses its grantmaking primarily on Jewish
organizations, temples, and schools. Of particular interest are centers and services
for the aging, education, human services, and international programs based in
Israel. Milton Jacobs, President,
423 Broadway Rm 706, Millbrae, CA 94030, (650) 589-5111

AMERICAN MUSLIM FUND (AMF)

Founded in 2016, in the midst of an explosion in regional and community-based
grantmaking, AMF characterizes itself as the nation's first Muslim community foundation. "We are looking to revolutionize the way Muslims give," said
cofounder Muhi Khwaja. "AMF supports Muslims in fulfilling their religious obli-
gations of zakat and philanthropy (sadaqa) by providing a streamlined vehicle for
charitable donations through donor-advised funds (DAFs)."
P.O. Box 1533, Fremont, CA 94538, (844) 426-3863

BLANCHE M. WALSH CHARITY TRUST

The Trust supports Roman Catholic charities, education, and social services delivery. Grants are awarded for one year, with the possible renewal of a second year.
Robert F. Murphy, Jr., TTEE, P.O. Box 238, Chelmsford, MA 01824,
(978) 454-5655

CALVIN INSTITUTE OF CHRISTIAN WORSHIP

The Institute's Vital Worship Grants seek to foster vital worship in congregations,
parishes, and other worshiping communities in North America. Priority is given
to projects that connect public worship to intergenerational faith formation and
Christian discipleship, a theme that can unfold in many facets of worship from
Bible reading to preaching to Baptism and the Lord's Supper, intercessory prayer,
congregational song, visual arts, and more.
1855 Knollcrest Circle , SE, Grand Rapids, MI 49546, (616) 526-6088

CARRIE ESTELLE DOHENY FOUNDATION

The Foundation funds nonprofits endeavoring to advance education, medi-
cine, and religion; to improve the health and welfare of the sick, aged, incapac-
itated; and to aid those in need. Educational funding is targeted toward inner
city Catholic schools as well as scholarship funds for Catholic high schools
and universities.
707 Wilshire Blvd, # 4960, Los Angeles, CA 90017, (213) 488-1122

CARYLON FOUNDATION

The Foundation awards general support grants to organizations of the Christian,
interdenominational, Jewish, and Presbyterian faiths. Higher education institu-

tions, health care organizations, international missions/ministries, medical centers, religious organizations, and temples receive support.
1917 Logan Avenue South, Minneapolis, MN 55403, (612) 596-3266

CATHOLIC CAMPAIGN FOR HUMAN DEVELOPMENT

The Campaign, a program of the United States Conference of Catholic Bishops, was begun in 1970 to fund projects such as "voter registration, community organizations, community-run schools, minority-owned cooperatives and credit unions, capital for industrial development and job training programs and setting up of rural cooperatives." The Campaign's Community Organizing grants support projects where poor and marginalized people join together to seek solutions to local problems and find ways to improve their lives and neighborhoods. Organizations must demonstrate a change from traditional approaches to poverty by attacking the basic causes of poverty and by effecting institutional change.
Catholic Charities, 1200 2nd Ave. South, Minneapolis, MN 55403
(651) 647-2588

CHARLES AND LYNN SCHUSTERMAN FAMILY FOUNDATION

The Foundation focuses its grantmaking on programs that seek to enrich and expand Jewish communities in the United States, Israel and the former Soviet Union. The Foundation also provides assistance to nonsectarian organizations dedicated to enhancing the quality of life in Tulsa, Okla., in the areas of education, child development, and community service.
110 West 7th Street, Tulsa, OK 74119, (918) 879-0209

CHARLES BRONFMAN PRIZE

Named for Charles Bronfman who spent a lifetime developing, implementing, and supporting initiatives that help to strengthen the unity of the Jewish people, the Prize is awarded in his honor. Bronfman spent his life investing in next generations to expand their knowledge and appreciation of their history, heritage, and cultural identity; and impacting on the direction of Jewish life and community.
445 Park Avenue, Suite 16A, New York, NY 10022, (212) 931-0127,
info@thecharlesbronfmanprize.org

CHATLOS FOUNDATION

The Foundation provides program support to Bible colleges, religious causes, liberal arts colleges, medical concerns with an emphasis on equipment, and social concerns. Less emphasis is given to requests for bricks and mortar, endowments, conferences and administration, and multi-year grants.
P.O. Box 915048, Longwood, FL 32791-5048, (407) 862-5077,
info@chatlos.org

CHRISTIAN AID MINISTRIES

The Organization's primary purpose is to be a trustworthy and efficient channel for Amish, Mennonite, and other conservative Anabaptist groups and individuals to minister to physical and spiritual needs of people around the world. Controlled

by a 10-member Board of Directors and operated by a six-member Executive Committee, the nonprofit aggregates contributions from concerned individuals and churches throughout the U.S., Canada, Mexico, and other countries.
P.O. Box 360, Berlin, OH 44610, (330) 893-2428

CONRAD N. HILTON FUND FOR SISTERS

The Fund supports the apostolic work of Roman Catholic sisters. Only vowed members of officially recognized Roman Catholic congregations of women religious are eligible to receive funding.
30440 Agoura Road, Agoura Hills, CA 91301

CORA FOUNDATION

This private, family Foundation's mission is to support Christian-based ministries that serve the spiritual, educational, and physical needs of people helping them come to know the love of Christ and live a dedicated Christian life. The Foundation provides support nationally for three primary programs: education, discipleship, and human services.
354 Brass Lantern Ct, Bozeman, MT 59715, (406) 586-2069

COVENANT FOUNDATION

The Foundation supports innovative programs in Jewish schools, agencies, community organizations, and other institutional settings. These grants enable creative Jewish educators to develop and implement outstanding approaches to Jewish education that are potentially replicable in other settings.
1270 Avenue of the Americas, Suite 304, New York, NY 10020,
(212) 245-3500, info@covenantfn.org

GHR FOUNDATION

The Foundation applies entrepreneurial creativity and universal catholic values in the areas of health, education, and global development. Founded by entrepreneurs Gerald A.
60 South 6th Street, Suite 2950, Minneapolis, MN 55402, (612) 440-2500, info@ghrfoundation.org

INTERO FOUNDATION

The Foundation, the philanthropic arm of Intero Real Estate, seeks to create community awareness by demonstrating good corporate citizenship. Its mission is to positively impact the growth and well-being of children through supporting organizations focused on assisting children (birth through age 17), their education, and personal development.
10275 N DE Anza Blvd, Cupertino , CA 95014

JEWISH HELPING HANDS

The Organization has launched its new Tikkun Olam grant program to advance the goal of inspiring and supporting tzedakah, justice, and righteousness around the world. This program will support projects that focus on reaching needy and

vulnerable populations in the United States and abroad, particularly those that
have been overlooked or marginalized.
90 Riverside Drive #4c, New York, NY 10024, (212) 712-2781,
rabbisoffin@jewishhelpinghands.org

JIM JOSEPH FOUNDATION

The Shimon Ben Joseph Foundation, commonly known as the Jim Joseph Foundation, is devoted exclusively to supporting the education of Jewish youth. About
60 percent of the awards focus on teens and young adults, ages 13 to 23, located in
the greater metropolitan areas of San Francisco, Boston, Los Angeles, and Washington D.C.
343 Sansome Street, Suite 550, San Francisco, CA 94104, (415) 658-8730

JOHN C. LASKO FOUNDATION TRUST

The Trust was created by John C. Lasko, the founder of Republic Tool and Die,
the largest privately-owned tool and die company in North America.
P.O. Box 1501, Pennington , NJ 08534, (312) 828-4154

JOHN TEMPLETON FOUNDATION

The Foundation, founded by the late Sr. John Templeton, has re-opened to new
funding requests.
300 Conshohocken State Road, Suite 500, West Conshohocken, PA 19428, (610)
941-2828

KALLIOPEIA FOUNDATION

The Foundation supports projects that contribute to a growing awareness of what
unifies, rather than divides, all people. Grantmaking is targeted at the work of people committed to holistic personal, community, and planetary transformation and
healing based on the recognition that we are at the core one humanity, expressing
itself through myriad ways and forms.
P.O. Box 151020, San Rafael, CA 94915, (415) 482-1043

KOCH FOUNDATION

The Foundation supports the evangelization efforts of the Catholic Church both
in the U.S. and worldwide.
4421 NW 39th Avenue, Building 1, Suite 1, Gainesville, FL 32606,
(352) 373-7491

KORET FOUNDATION

The Foundation was created in 1979 with money from the estates of Joseph and
Stephanie Koret, founders of the Koret of California women's sportswear line.
The Foundation focuses its grantmaking on the following areas: public policy initiatives, K-12 education reform, free-market economic expansion in Israel, and a
thriving Bay Area cultural landscape.
611 Front Street, San Francisco, CA 94111, (415) 882-7740

LILLY ENDOWMENT

The Endowment's National Clergy Renewal Program seeks to strengthen congregations by providing an opportunity for pastors to spend time away from the daily demands of parish ministry and engage in a period of renewal and reflection. Renewal times are not paid vacations, but times for intentional exploration and reflection. 2801 N. Meridian Street, Indianapolis, IN 46208, (317) 924-5471

LOUISVILLE INSTITUTE

The Institute's Pastoral Leadership Grant program supports research and reflection by pastors and academics on the conditions of contemporary Christian ministry, the nature of contemporary pastoral leadership in light of those conditions, and the character of pastoral excellence. Grant periods may range from nine weeks to nine months.
1044 Alta Vista Road, Louisville, KY 40205, (502) 992-5432

LOYOLA FOUNDATION

The Foundation supports overseas Catholic mission communities, primarily in less developed countries such as Africa, India, Central and South America. The Foundation awards grants for projects that demonstrate local support, have approval from the area diocesan ordinary, and show promise of becoming self-sustaining after completion.
10335 Democracy Lane, Suite 202, Fairfax, Virginia 22030, (571) 435-9401

LUCIUS N. LITTAUER FOUNDATION

The Foundation's interests involve supporting Judaica book funds and scholarly research on Jewish studies. The Foundation has also funded medical research with an emphasis on medical ethics and the environment.
220 Fifth Avenue, 19th floor, New York, NY 10001, (646) 237-5158,
Alan Divack, Program Director

MARY'S PENCE

The Organization awards its ministry grants to Catholic women working with projects aimed at self-empowerment among economically poor women and children throughout the Americas. Of particular interest are small ministries that emerge as women respond urgently to the needs in their own communities.
275 East 4th Street, Suite #510, St. Paul, MN 55101, (651) 788-9869,
inbox@maryspence.org

MAX AND ANNA LEVINSON FOUNDATION

The Foundation makes grants to activist organizations committed to developing a more just, caring, ecological, and sustainable world. The Foundation seeks people and organizations that combine idealism, dedication and genuine concern with rigorous analysis and strategic plans, and that foster a sense of social connection, mutual recognition, and solidarity.
P.O. Box 6309, Santa Fe, NM 87502, (505) 995-8802

MAX M. & MARJORIE S. FISHER FOUNDATION

The Foundation's mission is to enrich humanity by strengthening and empowering children and families in need. Priority is given to supporting the needs of and ensuring the future of the Jewish people and respecting its legacy and commitment to the Detroit, Mich., community.
Two Towne Square, Suite 920, Southfield, MI 48076, 248.415.1444

METANEXUS INSTITUTE ON RELIGION AND SCIENCE

The Local Societies Initiative is an Institute project with funding from the John Templeton Foundation. The Initiative provides three-year grants to fund start-up costs for dialogue groups exploring the dynamic interface between religion and science.
252 7th Ave #8x, New York, NY 10001

MUSTARD SEED FOUNDATION

The Foundation is a Christian family foundation inspired by the parable of the mustard seed. Grants are awarded to churches and Christian organizations world-wide.
7115 Leesburg Pike, Suite 304, Falls Church, VA 22043

OLDHAM LITTLE CHURCH FOUNDATION

The foundation focuses its grantmaking on small Evangelical Protestant churches with congregations ranging in size from 35 to 300. Established in 1949 in Texas by Morris Calvin Oldham, preference is given to completion grants for facility/building project needs in the form of repairs, renovations, and new construction projects.
24 Greenway Plaza, Suite 12022, Houston, TX 77046, (713) 275-1050

PORTICUS NORTH AMERICAN FOUNDATION

The Foundation seeks to enrich the life of the Catholic Church in the United States and Canada and to support the Church's outreach to the marginalized and dis-advantaged. Grantmaking is focused on three areas: renewal of the pastoral life of the Catholic Church; social service and outreach to disadvantaged families and communities; Catholic education and faith formation.
1001 Avenue of the Americas, Suite 1501, New York, NY 10018,
(212) 704-2300

PRESBYTERIAN COMMITTEE ON THE SELF DEVELOPMENT OF PEOPLE

The Committee is a ministry of the Presbyterian Church that's a partnership of love, justice, and empowerment reflecting the image of God who stands with all people. The Organization is prepared to establish partnerships with groups in the United States who are oppressed by poverty or social systems; want to take charge of their own lives; have organized or are organizing to do something about their own conditions; have decided that what they are going to do will produce long-

term changes for their lives and communities; and will control the programs they own and will benefit from them directly.
100 Witherspoon Street, Louisville, KY 40202, (800) 728-7228

PRESBYTERIAN COMMITTEE ON THE SELF-DEVELOPMENT OF PEOPLE

The Committee participates in the empowerment of economically poor, oppressed, and disadvantaged people who are seeking to change the structures that perpetuate poverty, oppression, and injustice. The Committee currently supports groups in the United States who are oppressed by poverty and social systems, want to take charge of their own lives, are organizing to do something about their own conditions, and have decided that what they are going to do will produce long-term changes in their lives or communities.
100 Witherspoon Street, Louisville, KY 40202, (800) 728-7228, info@pcusa.org

PRESBYTERIAN HUNGER PROGRAM

The Program, part of the ministry of the Presbyterian Church, provides grants in five areas: direct food relief, development assistance, public policy advocacy, education, and lifestyle integrity. The Program seeks to fulfill its mission through strategic grantmaking as well as Web educational and worship materials, partnership collaborations, and participatory programs.
100 Witherspoon Street, Louisville, KY 40202, (800) 728-7228

RASKOB FOUNDATION

Roman Catholic church organizations and missionary activities around the world are the Foundation's sole interest. The Foundation supports elementary and secondary education, community action and development, missionary activities, ministries (including youth and parish), health care, social concerns, AIDS victims, finance and development, and relief services.
10 Montchanin Rd, Greenville, DE 19807, Mailing Address: P.O. Box 4019 Wilmington, DE 19807, (302) 655-4440

RASKOB FOUNDATION FOR CATHOLIC ACTIVITIES

Roman Catholic church organizations and missionary activities around the world are the Foundation's sole interest. The Foundation supports elementary and secondary education, community action and development, missionary activities, ministries (including youth and parish), health care, social concerns, AIDS victims, finance and development, and relief services.
10 Montchanin Rd, Greenville, DE 19807, Mailing Address: P.O. Box 4019 Wilmington, DE 19807, (302) 655-4440

RIGHTEOUS PERSONS FOUNDATION

The Foundation, established by film director Steven Spielberg, focuses its grantmaking on projects that revitalize Jewish life, help youth to learn about Judaism,

and promote tolerance among all peoples of faith and ethnicities. Of particular interest are projects that explore new ideas and opportunities with a special emphasis on young people.
11400 W Olympic Blvd, Suite 550, Los Angeles, CA 90064, (310) 481-3513, grants@righteouspersons.org

SAJE FOUNDATION

The Foundation, established in 1999, focuses its grantmaking on supporting Christian organizations in the United States and in the developing world. The Foundation's principle partnerships are with organizations that effectively integrate their Christian faith in programs that assist people who suffer from material or spiritual poverty and injustice.
P.O. Box 809, Tustin, CA 92781, (714) 734-7808, info@sajefoundation.org

SHIMON BEN JOSEPH FOUNDATION

The Foundation was named for Joseph, a dedicated Jewish philanthropist who cared passionately about the education of Jewish children, youth, and young adults. The Foundation is dedicated exclusively to supporting Jewish education of youth and young adults in the United States.
343 Sansome Street, Suite 550, San Francisco, CA 94104, (415) 658-8730

SIEBERT LUTHERAN FOUNDATION

The Foundation funds Christian ministries identified with Lutheran churches and organizations. The Foundation enables the Lutheran community to be more collaborative, creative, and effective in how it shares the Word of God, how it educates and instills Christian values in youth, and how it serves people in need.
758 N. 27th Street, Milwaukee, WI 53208, (414) 269-2832, contactus@siebertfoundation.org

STEWARDSHIP FOUNDATION

The Foundation earmarks its funds to Christ-centered organizations that share their faith in Jesus Christ with people throughout the world. Funding is targeted at organizations that address leadership, poverty, reconciliation and justice, relational evangelism, cultural engagement, and organizational enhancement.
Mailing Address: Stewardship Foundation, P.O. Box 1278, Tacoma, WA 98401-1278, Street Address: Stewardship Foundation, 1145 Broadway, Suite 1500, Tacoma, WA 98402, (253) 620-1340

STRAKE FOUNDATION

The Foundation funds primarily Roman Catholic-affiliated associations including hospitals and higher and secondary educational institutions. The Foundation is also interested in adult basic education and literacy, museums, and arts and culture.
712 Main Street, Suite #3300, Houston, TX 77002

T. JAMES KAVANAGH FOUNDATION

The Foundation's grantmaking is focused on the Roman Catholic Church and religious associations along with support for U.S. Roman Catholic schools.
P.O. Box 1667, Hermitage, PA 16148, (724) 347-5215

TEN TALENTS FOUNDATION

The Foundation's mission statement guides its work. The Foundation focuses its grantmaking on churches and Christian organizations that are working in the areas of youth, education, human and social services, health, and the arts. 11701 Borman Drive, Saint Louis, MO 63146, (314) 994-9070

THE AARON STRAUS AND LILLIE STRAUS FOUNDATION

The Foundation's mission is to promote and sustain a strong Jewish community, both locally and worldwide. The Foundation also focuses its grantmaking on securing better futures for vulnerable children and their families by connecting them to opportunities which nurture their educational, social, economic, and physical well-being.
2 East Read Street, Suite 100, Baltimore, MD 21202, (410) 539-8308

THE BELL TRUST

The Trust provides temporary funding only to congregations associated with Churches of Christ. The Trust provides ongoing assistance to congregations in the support of ministers or missionaries.
11700 Preston Road, Suite 660-545, Dallas, TX 75230, (972) 788-4151,
barrypacker@belltrust.org

THE CHIAROSCURO FOUNDATION

The Foundation seeks to renew in the culture a deep awareness of the composite unity of our shared human nature. Members of the Catholic Foundation believe the truth of our dynamic body-soul existence is threatened by neo-gnostic impulses at play in our society especially in contemporary understandings of the gift of human life, the nature of familial relationships, how we die and remember the dead, and our life in eternity.
415 Madison Ave, 15th Floor, New York, NY 10017

THE CROWELL TRUST

The Trust was established by Henry Parsons Crowell, the founder of The Quaker Oats Company. It's dedicated to the teaching and active extension of the doctrines of Evangelical Christianity.
102 N Cascade, Suite 300, Colorado Springs, CO 80903, (719) 645-8119,
info@crowelltrust.org

THE FISHMAN FAMILY FOUNDATION

The Foundation focuses its grantmaking on Jewish culture, education, and the arts. It supports research, education, and cultural develop of and for the com-

munity; scholarships related to Jewish services, education, social, and community activities; medical and scientific research; educational grants and scholarships; and underserved local community programs.
426 E. Duarte Road, Monrovia, CA 91016

THE FORUM FOR THEOLOGICAL EXPLORATION

The Forum is a leadership incubator that inspires young people to make a difference in the world through Christian communities. Since its founding in 1954, the Forum has provided resources, events, networks, grants, and fellowships to cultivate tomorrow's leaders, pastors, and theological educators.
160 Clairemont Avenue, Suite 300, Decatur, GA 30030, (678) 369-6755

THE GENERATION TRUST

The Trust was created in 1985 in Ohio by John D. Beckett of the R.W.
P.O. Box 1868, Toledo, Ohio 43603, Contact: Marsha A. Manahan, Fifth Third Bank, (419) 259-6880

THE HENRY LUCE FOUNDATION

The foundation supports religion and theology as well as projects whose engagement extend into a variety of settings from religious communities and academic fields to activist networks and media venues.
51 Madison Avenue, 30th Floor, New York, NY 10010, (212) 489-7700

THE JACOB AND HILDA BLAUSTEIN FOUNDATION

The Foundation promotes social justice and human rights through its five program areas: Jewish life, strengthening Israeli democracy, health and mental health, educational opportunity, and human rights. Support is provided to organizations in the United States and abroad; however, the Jewish life one is the most general.
One South Street, Suite 2900, Baltimore MD 21202, (410) 347-7201

THE KENDRICK FOUNDATION

The Foundation was established to promote the dissemination of the Gospel of Jesus Christ. The majority of funds are distributed to charitable organizations that spread the Gospel of Jesus Christ in America by radio or television broadcasts or by such other medium (electronic or otherwise) as the trustees may deem to be a feasible approximation to radio or television broadcasting in light of then-existing technology.
11 West Main Street, Mooresville, IN 46158, (317) 831-1232

THE LUNDMAN FAMILY FOUNDATION

The Foundation funded by serial entrepreneur, Philip Lundman, focuses its grant-making on Christian organizations and agencies that cater to youth development and human services across the nation. It makes a limited amount of grants annually.
3631 W. Fredonia-Kohler Road, Fredonia, WI 53021, (262) 692-2416

THE MACLELLAN FOUNDATION

The Foundation's mission is to serve strategic international and national organizations committed to furthering the Kingdom of Christ and select local organizations, which foster the spiritual welfare of the community. Current giving strategies include: creating a revolution of generosity by providing consulting services to U.S.

THE MACLELLAN FOUNDATIONS

One of three Foundations (The Maclellan Foundation, the Robert L. Maclellan Foundation [NS4], and Kathrina H. Maclellan Foundation).
820 Broad Street, Suite # 300, Chattanooga, TN 37402, (423) 755-1366

THE RUPERT DUNKLAU FOUNDATION

The Foundation exists to glorify God and serve his gracious will by providing financial resources for the varied ministries related to the Lutheran tradition, especially the Lutheran Church-Missouri Synod, educational entities of the Lutheran Church, and appropriate projects that promote the welfare of mankind. Priority will be given to grant requests that help the Foundation realize its three main goals: faith strengthening, Lutheran education, and health and human care.
P.O. Box 22990, Lincoln, NE 68542, (402) 328-0370

THE TRUST FOR MEDITATION PROCESS

Founded in 1986 by a Christian layman with a deep commitment to meditation and a desire that others share his heritage, the Foundation's mission is to encourage meditation and contemplative practice among Christians. Grantmaking is focused on organizations that reclaim and teach Christian contemplative traditions, those that introduce meditation in the Christian community, or those that further understanding of contemplative practice in all spiritual traditions.
2751 Hennepin Ave. S., Suite #259, Minneapolis, MN 55408, (612) 554-7253

THE PILLARS FUND

Has also been engaged in "culture change" projects to counter anti-Muslim scaremongering (some of which conservative donors have abetted, as we've noted in the past). Pillars has brought in several liberal heavy-hitters to support that work, including the Nathan Cummings Foundation, the Ford Foundation, the W.K. Kellogg Foundation, the Open Society Foundations, and the McCormick Foundation.

THE WESTERMAN FOUNDATION

The Foundation focuses its grantmaking on educational institutions that emphasize Catholic education; Christian-based organizations, which promote family unity and values; and programs, which provide assistance to the poor and abused. Priority is given to Catholic education and organizations; educational projects and programs intended for community growth; and the enhancement of youth programs, which nurture the fundamental ideas of faith, charity, and the awareness of being fair.
3225 S. MacDill Ave, Suite 129-MB 233, Tampa, FL 33629, (813) 257-9477

TYNDALE HOUSE FOUNDATION
The Foundation is the philanthropic arm of the religious publishing company. It focuses its grantmaking on Christian and Protestant agencies and religious federated giving programs.
351 Executive Drive, Carol Stream, IL 60188, (630) 790-9532, foundation@tyndalehousefdn.org

UNITARIAN UNIVERSALIST ASSOCIATION OF CONGREGATIONS
The Organization's Fund for a Just Society accepts proposals from non-Unitarian Universalist groups in the U.S. and Canada for community organizing campaigns aimed at creating systemic change in the economic, social, and political structures that affect the lives of those who have been excluded from resources, power, and the right to determination.

UNITARIAN UNIVERSALIST FUNDING PROGRAM
The denominational grantmaking Program of the Unitarian Universalist Association, seeks to promote the influence of Unitarian Universalist principles by awarding funds to various organizations. The Program awards funds to both UU and non-UU projects and organizations.
24 Farnsworth Street, Boston, MA 02210, (617) 742-2100

UNITARIAN UNIVERSALIST VEATCH PROGRAM
The Program supports organizations that put Unitarian Universalists principles into practice. The Program funds Unitarian Universalist and community organizations working on a variety of issues in different parts of the country.
48 Shelter Rock Road, Manhasset, NY 11030, (516) 627-6560

VINE AND BRANCHES FOUNDATION
The Foundation exists to glorify God by supporting Christian charitable organizations that effectively build God's Kingdom. Built upon the Holy Scripture (John 15:5), the Foundation's mission is to promote Christianity and the building of God's Kingdom through partnerships with organizations that have the same beliefs and overt expression of Christian faith through their programs.
P.O .Box 2430, Brookfield, WI 53008, (262) 754-2799

VIRGINIA H. FARAH FOUNDATION
The Foundation makes grants for the maintenance and growth of the Orthodox Christian Church throughout the world with the goal of helping spread the Christian message while improving the quality of life on earth. Endowed by the daughter of an Orthodox priest, grants are awarded in the following topics: education, general, humanitarian, media and technology, mission and outreach, music and iconography, and publications.
P.O. Box 457, Wichita, KS 67201, (316) 682-1939

OTHER SOURCES OF FUNDRAISING

Many faith-based schools also receive money from the faiths with which they are affiliated; Tuition is of course a great source of income at some schools, but does not necessarily have to be the main or sole source of support from individuals. Individual donors, including family members who may already be paying tuition; close friends of families who attend the school; and parents, grandparents, and engaged community members may contribute to faith-based schools through direct gifts as well as participation in various fundraising campaigns. And please don't forget the all-important alumni donor base you should be building every year.

CORPORATIONS

Very few large corporations give to faith-based causes. In fact, in most instances they clearly state that they do not. Mid and small businesses, however have more flexibility and many of them could be a source for funding.

Whether it's individuals, foundations, or corporations who give to you, please remember to create a three-year fundraising plan. It will be your road map to generating your financial success.

SOCIAL MEDIA

Your website is the anchor for your social media outreach. The images you use and the stories you tell speak volumes about your work and professionalism. I have seen too many organizations with 1990's looking websites. It's a bad optic. Take time to put fresh eyes on your website and keep it looking current.

Social media can be effective if you have a plan. A wonderfully skilled and social media guru I have had the pleasure of working with, Arthur Gallow, recently shared these tips with me:

TIPS FOR CREATING A GREAT DIGITAL FUNDRAISING CAMPAIGN:

- Have a solid communications plan and a call to action (impact).

- Make it easy to give using a smart phone and have many payment options.

- Responsive website and easy navigation

- Prominent position for the donate button

- KISS: (Keep It Simple Saints) Make it easy and don't have a long form.

- Engage your supporters frequently by saying thank-you and asking them to share.

Evaluate your social media program with Key Performance Indicators:

- Donations

- Fans/Followers

- Impressions

- Website Traffic

On another note: Hashtags have POWER. What is yours? Social media can be a powerful fundraising tool for smaller gifts. Don't expect to meet all of your fundraising dollar goals through this vehicle. Major gifts will still require one-one in-person solicitations. With that cautionary note, go for it!

Questions for Discussion

1. What board members can be most helpful in using their contacts with corporations?

2. Who can be a resource for Foundation program officers?

3. Is our gala/golf tournament/luncheon the best way to raise the money we need?

4. Who should manage our social media presence and fundraising?

5. Are we ready to launch a major gift component to our annual giving program?

6. Are we relying too much on a foundation grant or on one event to raise money?

Steps to Take Right Now

1. Make a list of ten potential major gift donors and think of ways to cultivate relationships with them.

2. Identify the board members and who can be most helpful in your fundraising and ask them to serve on the Development Committee.

3. Take stock of how you are presently raising money.

4. Identify a social media expert (it might be a teenager in your community, or even in your house).

Bibliography for Chapter 10

Brown, M. Gasby. "Slow Relationships and the Art of Fundraising." June 2017. www.thegasbygroup.com

Wikipedia, "Slow Food Movement." Website accessed April 2017.

Greenfield, James. Original work from Association of Fundraising Professionals, 2011.

Rojc, Philip. "Looking To Grow: New Avenues Emerge for Muslim American Philanthropy." Inside Philanthropy May 30, 2018.

Society for Nonprofits: Funding the nonprofit world together: "Funding Alert: Religion."

Chapter Eleven

The Ultimate Gift: Planned Giving

They are like trees planted by streams of water, which yield their fruit in its season, and their leaves do not wither. In all that they do, they prosper.

—Psalm 1:3 (NKJV)

If you feel it is awkward to think or talk about money with potential planned givers, remember that planned giving is a matter of faith, and you can and should connect planned giving with your potential donor's faith in a way that is natural, appropriate, and authentic. Money should not be a taboo topic for people of faith. The Bible talks about money more than any other topic and stewardship is an essential component of all Abrahamic religions. There are many spiritual issues related to end-of-life planning. In fact, more gifts from estates go to religious organizations than any other type of organization.

Many people do not consider making a planned gift simply because they are not asked, are not informed about the ways they may give when they are asked, or it is not explained exactly why their financial support is important and what it will go towards. Potential donors might think that they have to be millionaires to be planned givers. By discussing planned giving with potential donors, your organization could be assisting future donors in living out their faith in a way that they may not have thought of before, or might have considered but been too afraid to try.

Planned giving is considered the ultimate donor gift in philanthropy. For organizations to be included in donors' financial and estate planning is often an untapped vehicle. However, it can be beneficial for both donors and your organization by providing donors with tax benefits as well as a means of living out their faith in a way they may not have thought of before. As a steward of your organization, it's your responsibility to explore the different ways that donors can give and provide them with the tools they need in order to make these gifts.

What is planned giving, and why it is important for your organization? When you hear the words "planned giving" you may think of very wealthy people with thick wallets and checkbooks. In reality, you do not need to search for millionaires to have a strong planned giving program. Research shows that planned giving has more to do with donor loyalty than wealth. For example, once someone decides to give to a charity as a bequest it is extremely unlikely, they will change their mind.

Look for people in your donor base, and compile a list to determine who would be a good candidate for a conversation about planned giving. Another effective way of organizing a plan giving program is to start a Legacy Gift Level in your fundraising pyramid.

In order to have an effective planned giving program you often have to provide potential planned givers with the resources they need to make a planned gift. Statistics show that although 42 percent of Americans have wills, only 9 percent have included charities. However, once people do include a charity, 97 percent of people do not revoke that provision from their will. That's good news.

In the 2019 Giving USA Report on Philanthropy in the United States, 9 percent of the $427 billion given to charity in 2018 came from bequests. That percentage is expected to increase as the boomer generation makes more bequests. It is up to your organization to make the ask and provide the potential donor with the support and resources they need to follow through. One way of doing this is inviting potential planned givers to a gathering with food and ask your banker, who usually has an estate planning program, to make a presentation. You could follow up with the attendees individually to gauge their interest at the time and cultivate an interest in a future bequest. Asking for the gift is a bit more complicated. More people should be involved, such as an attorney, financial advisor, family member, or others.

The financial benefit for your faith-based organization and the intangible benefits for donors who make contributions out of a desire rooted in their faith is also why planned giving is considered the ultimate gift.

Let's now focus on the different types of planned gifts. The information contained in this chapter is meant to be a top line summary of some types of planned gifts and is not a comprehensive description of all possible types of planned giving. If your organization seeks to enter into a planned giving agreement, you should secure advice from a responsible professional.

TYPES OF PLANNED GIFTS

Bequests

One type of planned gift is a bequest. A bequest is a provision in a will or estate plan that gives all or part of an estate to charity. Individuals who write a will have freedom regarding how much of their estate to give to charity. They can give a portion of their estate or its entirety to one or more charities. Naturally, a bequest will not be received by an organization until after the death of a donor. Because it's impossible to predict when a bequest will be received, it makes it difficult for charities to plan around it.

Actuarial tables using the parent's longevity, the donor's state of health, etc. can be helpful but certainty is not assured.

Charitable Gift Annuity

A charitable gift annuity is one of the simplest and most popular forms of planned gifts that can be made during the lifetime of a donor. With this gift, two transactions occur: the donor makes a gift to a charity and the charity provides the donor with an annuity. A charitable gift annuity involves a donor giving a charity a gift of cash, securities, or property in exchange for a contract for the charity to pay the donor a specified, fixed amount annuity for his or her life. This gift is irrevocable, and the charity maintains control of the gift and is responsible for paying income to the donor for his or her lifetime.

Split Interest Trusts

There are a number of split interest trusts that are used in planned giving. In this vehicle, there is both an asset, which may be money, financial investments, or property, as well as income, which is generated by the asset. One party will receive income from the asset for a particular period—often the lifetime of the donor of the asset—while the other party has full ownership of the asset after that period of time.

Charitable Remainder Trust

A charitable remainder trust pays out a specified annual amount to the donor or other designated beneficiaries for a specific number of years or a certain event occurs, which is often until the death of the donor. At the end of the trust the remaining assets are given to the charity. There are two different ways a charitable remainder trust may operate: a charitable remainder annuity trust and a charitable remainder unitrust.

Charitable Lead Trusts

A charitable lead trust operates in the opposite fashion of a charitable remainder trust. Over time the trust will pay a specified amount to the charity for a specified period of time or until a certain event occurs, which is often until the death of the donor. After that time the principal reverts to the donor or the donor's designated heirs if the donor is deceased. Whoever the principal amount reverts to will receive a charitable gift tax deduction. This trust is irrevocable, meaning it cannot be changed or undone once it is created.

Life Insurance

A donor may give a life insurance policy that has been paid in full to a charity. There are still some legal uncertainties regarding life insurance as planned giving. Be sure to consult with an estate planning professional.

Real Estate

A donor may give his or her home to a charity while retaining the right to live there for his or her life. The donor will receive an immediate tax deduction and the charity may sell the property upon his or her death.

PLANNED GIVING BEST PRACTICES

There are good examples of faith-based organizations that have used planned-giving models well. Volunteers of America has a website on planned giving that encourages potential donors by stating that many people wish they could make a gift of "startling significance," but do not think they can. The website addresses these concerns with news and information about planned giving and discusses types of planned gifts, donor stories, and provides guidance for people who choose to make a planned gift. They also provide a gift calculator at www.voa.org.

The YMCA of Silicon Valley created a comprehensive website for potential donors. The website is upbeat and includes a discussion about mutual dreams for the future. It has an interactive "Build Your Gift Planner" that operates like an online quiz, helping potential donors pick the best option for them. Potential donors can compare gift choices, read electronic brochures on particular giving options, and contact an attorney who is able to assist with planned giving. The website highlights online monthly feature articles about finances including the profile of a donor, tax law changes, a peace of mind checklist for end-of-life documents, an article about an estate planning blunder, and an article about listing the YMCA as a beneficiary for retirement plan assets or insurance policies.

Asbury University notes that more and more members of the Asbury family are benefitting from planned gifts. Their website discusses some planned gifts and has pictures and narratives about couples who enjoyed increased income and tax savings through gifts to Asbury. Professional advisors are provided free of charge to individuals who wish to make a gift to Asbury. This, and other strategies are great examples of how to market your planned giving program.

> **TIP:** *The best planned giving prospects are annual gift donors.*

People who make one large major gift to your organization may be unlikely to make a second gift like this, so it is important for your faith-based organization to cultivate a relationship with those individuals who give on a regular basis.

OTHER CONSIDERATIONS TO KEEP IN MIND

Look at your website. Is it Planned Gift friendly? In addition, there are probably people in your donor base that are sending you signals that they could be a candidate for a planned gift. Think about this questions and answer: Who do you think is the best prospect for planned giving: a one-time donor of $1,000 two years ago or someone who has given $100 every year for the past ten years? The answer is the latter. When cultivating donor relationships think about the individual circumstances of each planned giver to see what type of gift may be most appropriate for him or her. For example:

- Older retirees on fixed incomes who still give to charity may want to include the organization they care about the most in their will.

- Financially successful married couples in their forties to fifties who have children at home may also be good charitable bequest prospects, particularly if they are committed to the organization.

- Single females over sixty-five years in age who have out-lived their spouses can be good prospects for charitable gift annuities because they guarantee an income stream for the rest of their lives.

- African American Single Females, 50 years or older with incomes over 100,000 tend to be good candidates for planned giving cultivation.

- Wealthier people between their ages fifty to seventy who have made major gifts in the past can be good charitable remainder trust prospects. The trust could give them, or a beneficiary they designate such as their children, a steady income for a fixed period.

Scan your donor list to identify those who are likely to make a major gift, those who are likely to make some form of planned gift, and those who will do both. About 15 percent of prospects on your list could do both. These people tend to be those who know your charity the best.

YOUR PLANNED GIVING MESSAGING

Say it well, and say it often. When reaching out to potential planned givers make sure to send the right message to the right person. Keep it simple. It's confusing to send information about annuities and bequests at the same time, as that might be overwhelming. There is nothing wrong with using plain language and clear messages. In fact, I recommend it.

Your database of donors should be segmented according to who responds to a particular type of solicitation. For example, one person may respond well to phone calls while another may respond after receiving a mailing. Research shows that people who respond to direct mail solicitations tend to be good planned-giving prospects.

Your fundraising software will be invaluable here. It should allow you to keep track of anniversary dates, giving habits, and other information that will aid in identifying an individualized solicitation for potential planned giving donors. Your donor management systems also should allow you to keep track of communications you send to donors and when you sent them. Your annual fund team and your planned giving team should work together. If you are a smaller organization, the person managing your annual giving program will most likely manage the planned giving as well.

Planned giving is both an art and a science. There are many things your faith-based organization should consider before reaching out to potential planned givers. Once you are ready to launch a program it will be a great vehicle in your fundraising, especially if you are an organization with an annual giving track record of ten years or more.

Questions for Discussion

1. How soon should we launch a Planned Giving Program and who should manage it?

2. Are you able to see the giving history of your donors? Do you have a strong donor management system that allows you to track this information (giving history, anniversaries, birthdays, etc.)?

3. How are you currently cultivating donors? How do you thank them for gifts? What kind of information do you provide them about ways they can give?

4. Who are some professionals (accountants, attorneys, estate planning professionals, etc.) that you can reach out to regarding implementing a planned giving program at your faith-based organization?

Steps You Can Take Right Now

1. Make sure you have a Gift Acceptance Policy. If you don't, go online and see templates. Create one immediately.

2. Are there financial literacy programs at your faith-based organization? Can the church be a part of these conversations? Is there a way to do this as a part of the community? Can you partner with other organizations that are providing this kind of information?

3. Create a strong giving web page with resources that potential donors can use to make informed giving decisions.

4. Review your prospect list to identify individuals who may be good prospects for planned giving.

5. Prepare a plan for cultivating all donors. It's a good practice, but it's also a habit that can keep the organization in mind for planned giving inclusion.

Bibliography for Chapter 11

Asbury University. "Welcome to Asbury University Planned Giving." https://www.asbury.edu/about/offices/administration/development/making-gift/ (website accessed February, 10, 2011.

Ely, J. Richard Jr. "Planned Giving in Faith-Based Organizations: Making the Spirituality Real." National Committee on Planned Giving. October 13, 2007. PPT Directory.

Fritz, Joanne. "2 Popular Estate Planning Tools that Help Charities." The Balance Small Business. Updated April 16, 2018.

Henze, Lawrence. "Making Planned Giving Work for You." Blackbaud. October 2004.

Mercer, Eric. "Charitable Donations Through Planned Giving." Online Compendium of Federal and State Regulations for U.S. Nonprofit Organizations. 1999.

Volunteers of America. "Planned Giving." Website accessed February 10, 2011.

YMCA of Silicon Valley. "Planned Giving." Website accessed February 10, 2011.

YMCA of Santa Clara Valley, "Planned Giving" Website accessed February 10, 2011.

Chapter Twelve

Let Every Man (or Woman) Take a Beam: The Capital Campaign

And the sons of the prophets said to Elisha, 'See now, the place where we dwell with you is too small for us. Please, let us go to the Jordan, and let every man take a beam from there, and let us make there a place where we may dwell. So he answered, 'Go.' —2 Kings 6:1–2

Whether your capital campaign is bricks and mortar, special project, endowment, or program expansion, one thing is for sure: It is volunteer driven. You shouldn't attempt a capital campaign only using internal staff. The very nature of a capital campaign is that it is the largest amount of money you have tried to raise. You need large gifts to achieve success. I advocate that we should pray over everything. Making a decision to enter into a capital campaign requires much prayer and then planning.

Men and women of influence and affluence are essential to your successful execution. You should be able to start with members of your board, but just in case you ignored chapter 4 (shame on you), you will need to build a campaign planning committee made of volunteers and staff. I recommend that this committee have no more than eight members.

These members will be responsible for selecting the feasibility or campaign planning study consultant, helping to set the dollar goal, and beginning to identify potential lead gifts. The capital campaign should not look in any shape or form like a church "pass the plate" campaign.

Capital campaigns are a serious but lucrative fundraising process. And when conducted correctly without skipping too many steps, they can be a catalyst for stronger and more effective fundraising for your organization. Here are some dos and don'ts for planning your campaign.

DON'T

- start a campaign just because someone thinks it's a good idea

- announce a campaign too soon

- ignore the importance of the "Quiet Phase" (see below)

- launch a campaign without a campaign planning study

- choose a number out of the air just because you want to raise as much money as possible

- plan a campaign for more than five years

DO

- plan the campaign carefully

- use volunteers to lead the campaign

- use organizational leadership that is enthusiastic about the campaign

- have a good understanding with your finance department about how you count pledges and gifts

- secure your big gifts first

- have a communications plan

- make sure you have all the information you need from contractors and others if this is a brick-and-mortar or expansion campaign

- have a case for support

- have a gift acceptance policy

- encourage 100 percent board giving

- encourage 100 percent employee giving

- have a strategy for each lead and major gift donor

- have a gift range chart

- have a working dollar goal

- enlist volunteers to help make the ask

- have a recognition plan
- implement a good record keeping system
- have a good stewardship plan
- stay positive

THE QUIET PHASE

The Quiet Phase doesn't mean you don't tell anyone what you are doing, because how in the world would you raise money using that approach? The Quiet Phase merely means you haven't publicly announced the campaign to everyone. Wait until you have raised a significant amount of the campaign dollar goal before you have your kickoff event—I recommend 70 percent of your goal. It has been proven over and over that the last amount is the hardest to raise. By announcing too soon, you raise the public's expectations.

Isn't it far better to announce the campaign and then close it out within a year than to announce too soon and spend three to five years reaching the goal? It's a strategy that I have seen work, and I highly recommend it.

During the Quiet Phase you are going to organize the campaign committee, conduct the campaign planning study, hear the study report and act on it, select the campaign chair or cochairs, and set a dollar goal. You will also need to finalize the gift range chart, plan cultivation and solicitation of lead and major gifts, and plan the kickoff.

THE KICKOFF

The celebration to announce the campaign should be special. Use your creativity to make sure it is really impactful but not so lavish that it looks like you are spending money unwisely. Good kickoff events include:

- Public groundbreaking ceremony
- An existing high-profile event (make sure 60–70 percent is raised in the Quiet Phase)

- An event specially planned for the kickoff to recognize lead gifts and appeal to other major gift donors and general donors

Don't forget to include testimonials from people whose lives have been changed by your work at all public celebratory events.

THE PUBLIC PHASE

This is the time to use social media and digital fundraising like never before. Make sure that your social media images show your work and recipients of your work and not just a building. Choose hashtags that mean something to your organization. And by all means, use your website to communicate, communicate, and communicate. Let everyone know that you have 100 percent employee participation and 100 percent board participation.

CELEBRATE SUCCESS AND GOD'S GOODNESS

Successful campaigns are proud moments for nonprofit organization. You can say, "We did it!" Celebrate your accomplishment and celebrate loudly. Your donors will rejoice with you, and you will serve as a testimony to others that it can be done. Everyone plays a role in the success of a campaign, but God will get all of the glory for the things He has done.

HOW TO OVERCOME STAGNANT CAMPAIGNS

If, for some reason, the campaign doesn't reach its goal in the time period you have planned, please don't just keep going ad infinitum/nauseam. Reassess the goal. Announce success for phase one and plan for phase two, course correcting your mistakes and skipped steps. Donors will respect transparency and the need to recalibrate. A challenge or matching gift can also give a boost to a stalled campaign. Remember that a challenge gift is non-provisional, meaning you will receive the gift even if the challenge amount is not met. Not so with the matching gift. It is provisional and you will be expected to match that dollar goal. If you don't match it, the donor has the right to match only what you have raised during the specified period of time.

The capital campaign is the true test of your philanthropic strength. Having the right volunteer campaign leadership cannot be stressed enough.

Questions for Discussion

1. Why do you need a capital campaign?
2. Using standard practices, are we ready institutionally to mount a campaign? Why or why not?
3. What person could lead the campaign to success?
4. Should we include annual giving or not?
5. Who would you choose to be on a campaign core committee of approximately eight people?
6. Who would you use as a consultant?

Steps You Can Take Right Now

1. Revisit your organization's fundraising track record and make sure it is strong enough to launch a capital campaign.
2. Bring in a consultant to discuss all the aspects of the capital campaign and get initial advice.
3. Make sure you are thinking about how the campaign will impact your work to change lives, and not just about the bricks and mortar.
4. Study Genesis 11:3, 1 Kings 5:17, Haggai 1:8, Exodus 27:1, Psalm 127:1, 2, Samuel 7:2, Proverbs 24:3, Ephesians 4:12, 1 Kings 6:2, Matthew 7:24–27, 1 Kings 6:9, and 1 Kings 5:18.

Bibliography for Chapter 12

M. Gasby Brown. *7 Qualities of a Successful Capital Campaign* (2010). NPN Publishing

Chapter Thirteen

There Is Wisdom in Seeking Good Counsel: Choosing and Working with Consultants

Listen to advice and accept instruction,
that you may gain wisdom in the future.
Many are the plans in the mind of a man,
but it is the purpose of the Lord that will stand.

—Proverbs 19:20–21 (ESV)

There are a myriad ways in which an experienced nonprofit and philanthropic consultant can be helpful to your organization's growth and sustainability. Whether it is guiding the launch of an annual giving program, strategic planning facilitation, board development, or board orientation, conducting a campaign planning study, serving as campaign director for a capital campaign, or facilitating a staff or board retreat, good philanthropic consultants are worth their weight in gold.

I have seen too many failed instances where someone in an organization gets the bright idea that they can do it themselves. This myopic, non-biblical, and cost savings (cheap) approach has gotten many a nonprofit organization in trouble. They ultimately come back to ask for help anyway, so why not do it from the beginning? This is where a good board can make a lasting impact by providing the resources to hire experienced fundraising counsel. Corporations do it all the time. If there is a gap in knowledge and/or "hot spot" within the company, they bring in consultants who are super knowledgeable to help.

Nonprofit consultants must not be looked at as an extra pair of arms and legs to help do your day-to-day work. These consultants should be brought on for a specific period of time to increase your effectiveness through their expertise, experience, and wisdom, and respected as such. Carefully worded objectives and deliverables should be outlined at the very beginning.

While there is a donor bill of rights, fundraising and philanthropic consultants have rights as well. Consultants have the right to be:

1. Respected
2. Viewed as a thought partner
3. Valued for their expertise and experience
4. Candid with you about course correction strategies and tactics
5. A partner in your success

The following are some ways a consultant will be helpful to you.

Campaign Counsel

You might think that nonprofits that engage counsel to plan or help manage campaigns would be willing to collaborate with counsel, but that isn't always the case. The most successful campaigns have organizations willing to embrace a strategic thought partner who provides practical guidance on executing campaign best practices. Even for those organizations that have conducted campaigns before, this relationship can become key in directing their path to success.

Our ability to know and understand an organization's fundraising strengths and challenges but still be able to provide an "outsider's perspective," is important in order to:

• Manage volunteers.

- Coach those making the calls.

- Preserve the big picture and path to a successful end goal.

- Make sure an organization's fundraising program is better off following a campaign or the launch of an annual giving program, strategic planning, or board development than when it started. A capital campaign cannot survive with one person calling all of the shots. It is a team initiative that requires the support and commitment of several people.

In particular, a capital campaign needs specific individuals to ensure successful cohesion. Generally, these people will include:

- Members of your board of directors. Your entire board doesn't need to be on your capital campaign team, but make sure that you've enlisted the help of your key members before you start planning your capital campaign. Board members are often the most invested and well-connected individuals on your capital campaign team. They will be essential during the fundraising process.

- Staff members. Depending on your type of nonprofit, these team members may be faculty, heads of departments, or senior executives. It's a good idea to have a selection of people from different departments and areas for a well-rounded capital campaign team.

- Community volunteers. Your capital campaign team should not be comprised solely of organization members. Regular supporters of and advocates for your nonprofit are perfect candidates for your capital campaign team. These supporters may have benefited from your services and be alumni, previous hospital patients, or recipients of your goodwill.

Depending on the size of your committee and the scope of your capital campaign, you may need to break up your team into various subcommittees to help handle smaller or more detailed projects. Types of subcommittees that you could potentially create include:

- Government relations
- Loans and "bridge funding"
- Major gifts
- Funding from religious congregations
- Corporate donations
- In-kind donations
- Marketing
- Special events
- And more!

STRATEGIC PLANNING COUNSEL

Strategic planning is a process and should not result in merely a laundry list of to-dos (believe me I have seen my share of these misrepresenting a strategic plan). Rather, the strategic planning process should be methodical, smart, tangible, and realistic. A seasoned consultant can guide the process in a manner that is all inclusive and not just from the top down. An experienced facilitator will make the process seamless and sound.

BOARD DEVELOPMENT COUNSEL

Arthur Frantzreb said in his book *Not On This Board You Don't* "Great boards of charitable organizations don't just happen; they must be designed for greatness, constantly tuned and honed."

Boards are the linchpin and lifeblood of your nonprofit. A consultant can help you by conducting a board audit that reviews the bylaws and board orientation manual and interviews board members regarding their recruitment. A consultant can assist you in your board orientation, board knowledge regarding the organization, board participation and expected board financial support. Recommendations that result from the Board Audit are tremendously helpful in reactivating and reorganizing a board in a manner that is best for the organization, while maintaining good relationships. If staff takes the sole responsibility to uncover weaknesses and misunderstanding of board roles, it can create an awkward future working relationship.

EXECUTIVE COACHING

Whether it is the CEO, development staff, or a new board chair, an experienced consultant can be a valuable thought partner and best practices coach to help strengthen the skills of these important roles in your organization. This type of coaching can often be done virtually through technology similar to Skype and, at all times, will remain confidential. This type of coaching can be short- or long-term, and is usually very effective.

DEVELOPMENT STAFF COUNSEL

This type of fundraising counsel is usually for a new and young development staff. Sessions with the consultant can take place through a "boot camp," staff retreat, or regularly scheduled meetings over a period of time (anywhere from three to twelve months).

I know. You are probably asking yourself how to find the right fit for this position. This is a decision that requires research and wisdom because there is a financial investment involved here. Start with these steps:

1. Obtain referrals from other organizations like yours, if possible.
2. Interview several consultants.

3. Make sure their values align with yours.

4. Ask for references.

5. Get a clear sense of their expertise and experience.

6. Request examples of their work.

Questions for Discussion

1. Does my organization need outside help in thinking through our next steps for success?

2. How would I best benefit as a leader from a consultant?

3. Is it worth it?

Steps You Can Take Right Away

1. Begin to think hard about how an outside consultant could help you in planning.

2. Evaluate your current team.

3. Be honest about your needs.

Bibliography for Chapter 13

Panas, Jerold. Institute for Charitable Giving. Institute website accessed March 2017.

Frantzreb, Arthur. *Not on This Board You Don't: Making Your Trustees More Effective.* Bonus Books, Inc., 1997.

Chapter Fourteen

Meeting Economic Challenges: Prayer Changes Things . . . and So Does Time

*There is a time for everything,
and a season for every activity under the heavens.*
—Ecclesiastes 3:1 (NIV)

Change. It can be a scary thought. The "what if" questions that plague many faith-based nonprofit leaders usually stem from money. When we all received the invitation to participate in the 2008 recession, we all had to RSVP. Some nonprofit organizations never recovered, while others did well in spite of the economic downturn. What made the difference?

While we saw many organizations recover, partner, and dissolve during that time, there are always other factors that organizations and leaders must face, including changing US leadership. If the president of the United States and Congress understand and value the need for nonprofits, we are in good shape. But that will not always be the case. Federal budget cuts for services and tax implications for charitable giving are just a few of the challenges regarding fundraising and nonprofit operations that we may need to confront. A handful of congressional representatives want nonprofits to start a different way of "paying their freight."

ON THE LOCAL LEVEL

In 2017 a Massachusetts State Representative proposed that some Massachusetts nonprofits should be forced to pay property taxes. He based his proposal on what he called "excessive salaries for nonprofit leaders."

On the National Level

US Senator Chuck Grassley is also aiming to change the taxation of nonprofits. Grassley is chairman of the Senate Finance Committee and member of the US Congress Joint Committee on Taxation. Here's what he said in a press release in 2011:

> The federal tax laws governing nonprofit organizations have been mostly untouched since America sent a man to the moon. And while the nonprofit sector has blazed a trail of good deeds and good works for mankind since 1969, the temptation to exploit charities for personal gain has attracted more than a few bad actors to take a bite at the tax-exempt apple.
>
> As chairman of the tax-writing Senate Finance Committee, I take seriously my constitutional responsibilities to protect the public purse. From simplifying the tax code to strengthening entitlements for future generations, securing tax relief for hardworking Americans and enhancing private pensions and personal savings opportunities, I advance public policies that treat taxpayers fair and square.
>
> That to-do list includes my efforts to ensure the nation's tax laws strengthen Americans' longstanding tradition of charitable giving and protect taxpayers from subsidizing wrongdoers who misuse nonprofits for their own good.
>
> Just as Congress has acted in the public interest to protect shareholders and workers from corporate mismanagement, so too must Congress demand transparency, accountability and good governance from the nonprofit sector.
>
> Nonprofit organizations must earn the privilege to keep their tax-exempt status. Tightening the rules and regulations governing the nonprofit sector will help repair the breach of trust that threatens to tarnish even the most reputable charities in America.

Working with more than 100 charitable groups, I have developed a legislative package of reforms to strengthen America's deeply rooted tradition of charitable giving and to renew the federal government's covenant with philanthropic good works for the 21st century. Based on my congressional investigation to track the abuse and misuse of tax-exempt organizations, I have identified key areas of concern, including:

- Excessive compensation perks, pay and sweetheart deals involving officers and directors
- Nonprofit groups that act more like for-profit businesses than charities
- Inappropriate political activity
- Lack of financial transparency and accountability to donors
- Nonprofit hospitals that do not provide adequate charity care and community benefits
- Tax-exempt organizations fronting as tax-shelters
- Donor-advised funds and supporting organizations being used by the wealthy to protect business assets and take big charitable tax deductions with little or no money actually going to public charities
- Charitable boards that are not engaged in their fiduciary responsibilities to ensure that the charity is operated appropriately and responsibly

I'm not so naive as to believe that enacting a new law will fix these problems overnight, but it's also clear that merely enforcing current laws won't get the job done. That's why I'm working in cooperation with the nonprofit sector and the Internal Revenue Service to build a consensus for balanced, comprehensive reforms that will help weed out bad actors and bad practices that give the non-profit sector a black eye.

Enhancing charitable-giving tax incentives, raising standards for stronger internal financial controls, enacting new laws that reflect today's environment, and overseeing agile enforcement by the IRS would go a long way to strengthen the public's faith and trust in charitable organizations.

Tightening the reins on the nonprofit sector today will make it better prepared to do even greater good for the public good tomorrow. And if more and more entrepreneurs follow in the footsteps of Warren Buffett and give away their fortunes to help the less fortunate, the nonprofit sector will be ready and able to serve better the unmet needs of society.

New Tax Laws

2018 was a complex year for nonprofits. Although Americans gave $427.71 billion according to the Giving USA 2019 Report, this number was down from 2017 by 1.7 percent when adjusted for inflation. The stock market decline was a factor, but the new tax laws were the major reason. More than 45 million households itemized deductions in 2016. Countless studies indicate a drop to 16–20 million households because the incentives for charitable giving have been reduced. A bigger drop is expected for 2019.

I recently ran into Brian Flahaven, Senior Director for Advocacy Council for Advancement and Support of Education (CASE) and Jason Lee, Chief Advocacy and Strategy Officer and General Counsel at the Association of Fundraising Professionals (AFP). They shared the following information with me:

> The Potential Loss in Charitable Donations Per Year due to Tax Reform according to the following organizations:
>
> $16–17 billion (2018) – American Enterprise Institute (AEI)

$13.2 billion annually – Independent Sector/Lilly Family School of Philanthropy

$12–20 billion annually – Tax Policy Center

Why Would This Happen?

- People who itemized provided 82 percent of total individual giving in 2016 giving in USA.

- The enacted tax reform legislation increased the standard deduction and likely will reduce those who itemize from 33.3 percent of all taxpayers to 5 percent–10 percent (up to 30 million people will no longer itemize).

- Taxpayers will see the impact of tax reform for the first time in their 2018 taxes. Giving behaviors may subsequently shift in 2019 and 2020 after a couple of tax cycles.

- Strategies such as gift "bundling," the use of donor advised funds, and other options may supplant traditional annual giving in future years.

More Tax Challenges

The Unrelated Business Income Tax (UBIT) is proving to be a burden for tax-exempt groups, including churches and small charities that have little or no experience dealing with the Internal Revenue Service (IRS) and insufficient guidance on how to calculate the value of parking and other benefits provided to their employees, according to Lauren Precker, social communications and strategy manager at American Society of Association Executives (ASAE).

A report commissioned by Independent Sector (IS) issued January 24, 2019 shows that the new tax will annually divert an average of $12,000 from each nonprofit's mission. About ten percent of nonprofits are considering dropping transportation and parking benefits entirely, although these employer-provided benefits are mandated in some metropolitan areas like Washington, DC, New York, and San Francisco.

"These (UBIT) provisions divert precious funds away from missions and the communities who need it most," said Daniel J. Cardinali, president and CEO of IS. "We heard from nonprofit leaders who were concerned about the impact of these taxes and confused about how they were going to be implemented. We commissioned this research to educate the nonprofit community and urge Congress to quickly repeal these two provisions."

Check with the IRS guidelines to make sure you are in compliance. When you conduct your annual audit with an outside accounting firm this should be an area of examination. If you have a Finance Committee of your board, they should be charged with exploring all of the tax laws that pertain to your operation.

Examples of employee benefits that would be subject to taxation if the LIFT for Charities Act is not adopted include parking spots, provided meals, and transportation benefits. For example, many Goodwill centers offer transportation to employees.

DONOR-ADVISED FUNDS (DAFS)

The landscape for DAFs is changing and growing. DAFs have proliferated over the past five years at an incredible rate. More donors are using them to make their charitable gifts.

There are a few things to remember:

The donor receives a thank you and other acknowledgment but NOT a receipt. When they contributed to their DAF, they received an immediate tax write off.

DAFs can be used to purchase a table for a charitable event, but the donor cannot sit at that table secured with DAF money. And they must purchase separate tickets or a table (not using their DAF) if they want to attend.

Please note that as of this writing a few new laws concerning DAFs are being introduced that will favor nonprofits if adopted. Keep an eye on the DAF landscape by reading philanthropy trade magazines such as *The Chronicle of Philanthropy, Advancing Philanthropy* and podcasts produced by The Fund Raising School (TFRS).

Impact Investing

This is a new concept that some foundations are embracing as a way to merge business interests with philanthropy. If there is a business opportunity through the services a nonprofit offers, the service may be a candidate. For example, NONPROFIT X may have a thrift store attached to its business model. Impact investors who have had vast retail experience may offer investment support for the thrift store in exchange for providing expertise on how to grow the thrift store and make more money. In exchange, the investor will ask for a minimum of three percent (and higher) return on investment (ROI). The nonprofit's mission benefits from the growth and the investor get their ROI.

As clean as it may sound, there are layers of understanding and IRS implications that are being worked out, so keep an eye on this one as well.

Questions for Discussion

1. How have the new tax laws impacted our fundraising?
2. Do we need to buffer for a downturn in the economy? Why or why not?
3. Does our three-year strategic plan include changes to the economic landscape?
4. Should we have a crisis communication plan in place?
5. What should we know about Donor-Advised Funds (pros and cons)?
6. Is Impact Investing something we need to know more about?

Steps You Can Take Right Now

1. Monitor the new tax law effects on philanthropy by following articles in philanthropic trade publications and the reports and podcasts from The Fund Raising School (TFRS) at Indiana University's Lilly Family School of Philanthropy and *The Chronicle of Philanthropy*.

2. Make sure you have an accountant who is keeping up with tax code trends.

3. Join the Association of Fundraising Professionals.

4. Explore Impact Investing as a way to move your organization forward.

5. Ask for a meeting with your banker to help you understand Donor-Advised Funds.

6. Plan for "rainy days" with your board.

Bibliography for Chapter 14

Pfeiffer, Sacha and staff. *Boston Globe* Spotlight team stories. March 24, 2017. Accessed online September 2018.

Cardinali Daniel J. "The New Tax Law: How It Will Impact Your Nonprofit Organization and 5 Solutions to Mitigate Your Risk." Social Impact Architects. Independent Sector.org. Accessed online April 2019.

Giving USA Foundation 2019. A partnership between The Giving Institute and the Indiana University Lilly Family School of Philanthropy. Accessed June 2019.

Chapter Fifteen

Traits of Good Leaders of Faith-Based Nonprofits: Think on These Things

For as he thinks in his heart, so is he.
—Proverbs 23:7 (NKJV)

WHAT MAKES A LEADER?

The basic qualities that make a leader—authority and strength—may seem to contradict the humility associated with people of faith. These contradictions need to be acknowledged and, indeed, embraced. The values that drive the mission of the organization can help you balance the competing expectations of staff, board, and other stakeholders. It is important to realize it's possible to be a strong leader while maintaining your humility and spiritual integrity. In fact, without those qualities, leadership is a useless, even dangerous, thing.

About fifteen salient qualities come to mind when I hear the word *leader*. Then I ask myself about the qualities that come to mind when I think of a leader of a faith-based organization. I have personally seen people in leadership positions who have humility and I've seen those in charge with a pretense of humility—and also have seen heads of organizations who are downright pompous. Can a leader be truly powerful *and* modest and humble? I know what the answer is: absolutely!

Certainly, there are a myriad of lists that serve as checklists for good leadership. My nonprofit experience of over thirty years has exposed me to all types of leaders—the great, the good, the bad, and the ugly. The great ones at faith-based nonprofits really stand out for me as shining examples of leadership.

Jesus had twelve disciples, and there were twelve tribes of Israel. In that spirit I am offering my top 12 qualities of a great leader of a faith-based nonprofit:

1. *Has passion for the mission:* Without this crucial element a leader of a faith-based nonprofit organization will always be mediocre at best. Mediocre is unacceptable in a leader.

2. *Is well-Informed:* Read, read, read information about the sector you are serving and about others who are achieving results for inspiration.

3. *Inspires others:* Unless you have had that surgery called a "Charisma Bypass," there is no excuse to not be an inspiration through your vision, work ethic, humility, and sense of fairness to everyone in your organization. Articulate it often.

4. *Has visionary instincts:* Leaders don't manage; they think about the future and set about doing something about it now. There is a stark difference between a placeholder and a change-maker leader. Be the latter.

5. *Hears God's voice:* Many people will have opinions, but whose report will you believe? Take devotion time to pray and listen as you are making final decisions. Believe the report of the Lord.

6. *Has good advisors:* Wise counsel (people who walk the talk) is always good. It helps to look at all sides of an issue. Remember what Aaron said to Moses when he had taken on too much in leading the children of Israel.

7. *Understands what good fundraising is all about:* Knowledge about the art and science of fundraising is

critical to your success as a leader. Remember: "No money, no mission" should be your mantra when it comes to fundraising. Fifty percent of your time should be spent on fundraising. Get training or coaching if you need it; most good leaders do.

8. ***Takes risks:*** Bold ideas can be scary. Look at some of the pushback God received from many of those he used to make change: Abraham, Jonah, Peter, Moses, Jeremiah, Nehemiah, Elijah, and many others. They took risks and it paid off.

9. ***Strives for excellence and seeks feedback to achieve it:*** How did we do? A debriefing after events, speaking engagements, fundraising visits, staff meetings, and cultivation opportunities will speak volumes about your willingness to grow and achieve excellence. Don't be one of those leaders who only wants to hear "good news" from everyone. Mediocrity and failure are the results of not listening to transparent and meaningful feedback. Demand excellence. According to Colossians 3:23, "And whatever you do, do [it] heartily, as to the Lord, and not unto men." Attention to detail is also a leader's calling.

10. ***Exudes confidence:*** Frayed collars, a steady stream of bohemian dresses, and ill-fitting clothes do not engender confidence with your external stakeholders. Additionally, staff wants to feel proud of their leader, not embarrassed. A recent study revealed that donors who were given photos of nonprofit leaders without knowing what organization they represented picked the ones that were dressed more casually—a neat open collar and jacket for men, and dark suits with minimal jewelry for women. Your cause also dictates your appearance. Choose carefully, look confident, and lead the way!

11. ***Uses connections well:*** The majority of your time should not be spent sitting at your desk, but rather out in the community and beyond. Your ability to connect with people of influence and affluence cannot be overemphasized. By the way, this is not the opportunity to boast about who you know, but to quietly, strategically, methodically, and genuinely advance the mission of your organization through the network you are developing or have developed.

12. ***Understands the need for systems:*** Let's face it, being a visionary leader doesn't automatically come with an organized system, so get help! By getting the right help (an executive assistant), your scheduling, follow-through on important meetings, planning, and so on will be so much more efficient. Remember that everything that is consistently repeated requires a system. Make sure systems are in place.

Questions for Discussion

1. Which of the top twelve traits is your strongest?
2. Which of the top twelve needs work on your part?
3. Which present-day leader inspires you most?
4. Which leaders from the Bible do you get the most inspiration and why?
5. What is your Achilles' heel—the flaw or sin to which you're most susceptible? How will you work to mitigate this risk?

Steps You Can Take Right Now

1. Look at the 360-degree performance evaluation system and consider adopting it for your organization. This system will allow you, as the leader, to receive candid feedback.

2. What software systems are in place to keep you organized?

3. Examine your vision. Is it just the mission warmed over or is it truly aspirational?

4. Gather a few trusted advisors to help you through the twelve traits checklist.

5. From among the three decisions you considered in the previous step, which one least embodies your deeply held values? How can you make it right tomorrow? Can you seek forgiveness?

Bibliography for Chapter 15

David Bonbright, CEO and Founder of Keystone Accountability, with Denver Frederick on The Business of Giving. January 28, 2016. https://denverfrederick.wordpress.com/2016/01/28/david-bonbright-keystone-accountability/

M. Gasby Brown. *Leadership with Impact.*

FaithSearch Partners. "Executive Onboarding Checklist for Faith-Based Nonprofits: 9 Keys to Equipping New Leaders in Nonprofit Organizations with Faith-Based Missions." http://faithsearchpartners.com/executive-onboarding-checklist-for-nonprofits/

John Maxwell. *3 Things Successful People Do.* Thomas Nelson, 2016.

"15 Outstanding Questions Leaders Ask Themselves Every Day." http://yscouts.com/executive/15-outstanding-questions-leaders-ask-every-day/

Credits for Photographs

Index

About the Author

photo by Jackie Hicks

M. Gasby Brown, Founder & CEO of Have Faith Institute, has a passion for nonprofits that is beyond the norm. She believes strongly in the power of a well-run nonprofit organization. She is also fully aware that solid and innovative fundraising are keys to project and organizational success. In her cabinet-level experiences as an executive in organizations such as Greenpeace, National Urban League, and The Washington National Opera, she has been instrumental in restructuring and reenergizing board and constituent participation as well as fundraising.

Gasby graduated from Harvard University's Kennedy School where she earned a master's degree in Public Administration (MPA). She has a long list of brand name and not-so-brand-name clients ranging from high profile universities and churches to grass-roots service organizations and medical foundations. As a faculty member of the esteemed The Fund Raising School at Indiana University's Lilly Family School of Philanthropy, she has trained fundraising professionals representing every conceivable nonprofit organization, both large and small. Her one-on-one consultations tied to those trainings have ranged from Oxford University in England to Moi University in Kenya.

Gasby Brown is a sought after consultant, speaker, and trainer in the nonprofit world. She is the author of *Art of Praise, 7 Fatal Flaws of Nonprofit Boards and How to Fix Them, Leadership with Impact, and 7 Successful Qualities for Capital Campaigns*. She is on the adjunct faculty roster of the Lake Institute's training for the Executive Certificate in Religious Fundraising (ECRF) at Indiana University's Lilly Family School of Philanthropy.

Gasby resides in Atlanta, Georgia, with her husband and partner, Kenneth R. Brown.

For more information, go to
http://www.thegasbygroup.com/bio.html